I0555247

heartbundance

The Art & Science of Healing
After Heartbreak

Heartbundance: The Art & Science of Healing After Heartbreak Through Trauma-Informed Manifestation

2025 fEMPOWER Press Trade Paperback Edition
Copyright © 2025 DIANE COLE

All Rights Reserved. No part of this book can be scanned, distributed, or copied without permission. This book or any portion thereof may not be reproduced or used in any manner whatsoever without the express written permission of the publisher at media@fempower.pub—except for the use of brief quotations in a book review.

The author has made every effort to ensure the accuracy of the information within this book was correct at time of publication. The author does not assume and hereby disclaims any liability to any party for any loss, damage, or disruption caused by errors or omissions, whether such errors or omissions result from accident, negligence, or any other cause.

Some names and identifying details have been changed to protect the privacy of those discussed.

This book is not intended to be a substitute for the medical advice of a licensed physician. The reader should consult with their doctor in any matters relating to their health.

The publisher is not responsible for websites (or their content) that are not owned by the publisher.

Published in Canada, for Global Distribution by fEMPOWER Publications
www.fempower.pub | For more information email: media@fempower.pub

ISBN trade paperback: 978-1-998721-24-5
Ebook: 978-1-998721-25-2

To order additional copies of this book: media@fempower.pub

heartbundance

The Art & Science of Healing
After Heartbreak

THROUGH TRAUMA-INFORMED MANIFESTATION

Diane Cole

*This is dedicated to the people who taught me
the most about love, devotion, and thriving in hardship.*

*My parents, for showing me
what a beautiful marriage looks like.*

*My husband, for loving me so deeply
that I shine like a diamond in the sun.*

*And my children, for helping my heart grow
ten times its original size.*

contents

part III: claiming your manifestation mind

There's a moment when the lights
turn on and you realize you deserve
so much more than this.

the moment it all clicked

I'll never forget the moment everything finally clicked for me. I was sitting on a campus bench in the early 2000s, just a college student trying to make sense of my world, when he looked at me with chilling, eerie calm and said I was "so crazy that no one else could possibly tolerate" me but him.

And just like that, I realized that it wasn't true. After five years of emotional abuse and being intentionally misled, the fog lifted and I could see clearly.

In an instant, years of confusion, self-doubt, and quiet suffering snapped into focus. I realized that the things he told me, and things he claimed no one else would be honest enough to say, were never truths. They were weapons.

More accurately, they were carefully chosen weapons disguised as words meant to reshape the way I saw myself. Weapons meant to mold me into someone smaller, more dependent, and easier to control. The truth is, I wasn't crazy. He was making me feel crazy. The truth is, I was never unlovable. He was isolating me from everyone who loved me, then convinced me they didn't care.

It felt like someone flipped a switch and flooded the room with light. Suddenly every manipulation, every subtle dig cloaked as concern, every act of control pretending to be love was exposed. I could see it all. The clarity was so sudden and unexpected that it actually brought me a ton of relief. Confusion was replaced with certainty. Unease was replaced by a feeling of groundedness. And then another unexpected thing happened: I laughed. Not out of joy, but from this newfound liberation that suddenly arrived.

My laughter at his manipulation was not my usual reaction, and it wasn't what he was expecting at all. He looked confused and asked what was so funny with thinly veiled irritation in his voice. For a moment, I considered telling him that I knew what he was doing. I wanted to explain why he was full of it and give him proof that I wasn't crazy, just a college student with worries like everyone else, and he could save his breath. But this clarity ushered in a new wave of understanding.

I now knew that he understood all that already. I didn't have to explain to him about how misleading and manipulative he was. So, I simply said, "Nothing," then walked away. There was no use in going back and forth. He would never admit what he was doing. He would simply twist my words and gaslight me again. But I didn't need his validation anymore. Saying nothing at all was my first step back to myself.

At the time I was only twenty-two. When I look back, I was just a little girl still. I was unsure of myself, confused, and downtrodden after five long years of emotional abuse. When that moment of clarity happened, it felt like everything clicked at once, but when I look back now, I can see that I was finally beginning to pick up the broken pieces of my spirit bit by bit before this happened. Yet, that moment was the true beginning. I was returning to the truth. I was finally able to do something different in service of me and not in service of a relationship that caused me so much invisible pain.

Now, I see these dynamics so clearly. Twenty years later, and many years of walking hand in hand with other survivors, has given me a lot of insight into how emotional abusers operate. They don't just hurt you. They steal parts of you. They target your power, your confidence, and your potential. And not because you're weak but because your light threatens them. They tear you down so you'll stay. But healthy love doesn't shrink you. It expands you. It empowers you.

All of us who've survived emotional abuse carry invisible scars. But we also carry the strength it took, and takes, to survive. Any form of abuse in relationships is traumatic, but there are hidden scars in quietly toxic relationships too that can have a similar, destructive impact. I've had the privilege of walking alongside survivors of codependent relationships, survivors of relationships with emotionally immature partners, and survivors of toxic parents who didn't immediately identify as abuse survivors but experienced harmful relationship dynamics that hurt their spirit, shaped their identity, and imprisoned their confidence.

All of us deserve more than just survival. We deserve healing. Real, deep, soul-level healing. The kind that doesn't just patch the wound but helps unravel the twisted beliefs the abuser or unhealthy relationship forced us to accept. The kind that helps us come home to ourselves. The empowered, intuitive, worthy self that was always there underneath it all.

That's what *Heartbundance* is about.

It's a sacred three-part process: healing the injury of love trauma, dismantling the false identities that were created by the experience, and cultivating a manifestation mind that's not influenced by the love trauma.

Once that false story loses its grip, your real voice returns. Your intuition awakens. And with that, you can finally release the resistance standing between the life you have now and the life you're meant to create.

We hear so much these days about healing, trauma, and manifestation. But here's the truth that's often left out: For survivors of love trauma, it's not as simple as reciting affirmations or visualizing a new future. Because when someone (or a toxic relationship itself) has systematically made you believe that you're powerless or unworthy, it's not just a belief—it becomes a lens through which you see the world.

And no amount of positive thinking will rewrite a narrative that was embedded in your nervous system and spirit. But that doesn't mean you can't rewrite it. It just means *our path is different*. And it works. I know because I've walked it myself. I know because I've stood side-by-side with countless survivors, guiding them back to their truth, helping them heal the wound *and* unravel the illusion caused by love trauma.

As they unraveled those illusions, they didn't just feel better. They *became* clearer. Freer. Stronger. They opened the door to the version of themselves that was always waiting, emerging capable, empowered, and ready to manifest a new chapter from a place of truth.

That's what's waiting for you too.

You deserve to heal. You deserve to break free of the chains that were crafted to keep you small. **And you deserve not just to heal but to rise into the life you were always meant to have.** I'm here to walk that path with you. Let's get started.

Healing relationship wounds
and restoring your sense of worthiness
are the keys to an abundant life.

what is heartbundance?

Let's fast-forward more than twenty years. I grew up, earned a master's degree in mental health counseling, became a licensed psychotherapist, and dedicated my career to trauma recovery. Eventually, I started to focus on helping people heal from emotionally abusive relationships and love trauma in general.

Over the years, I've had the privilege of sitting with hundreds of clients who, despite their intelligence, resilience, and effort, felt stuck. They were cut off from their desires, disconnected from their dreams, and confused about why nothing seemed to shift no matter how hard they tried. And almost every time, when someone shares that nothing ever works out for them, or that they feel like the Universe has forgotten them, I ask them a simple but powerful question:

"How were you loved?"

I don't only want to know how they were loved romantically, but in all the ways that someone is loved. I want to know about their earliest experiences of love and relationships. I want to know about their parents, caregivers, childhood friendships, and first romantic relationships. The ones that left the deepest impressions. The ones that shaped how they see themselves and what they believe they deserve.

There's a direct, undeniable connection between how we were loved and how we feel about our worthiness, our capacity to receive, and ultimately, our ability to create the lives we want.

There is a ton of variety in the responses I get to this question. Some people blink in surprise when I ask. Others burst into tears. Intuitively, many of us already know: When we've been hurt in love (especially in subtle, manipulative, inconsistent, or dismissive ways), the experience imprints something deep inside us. And that imprint doesn't just affect how we love others. It quietly shapes how we love ourselves, how we dream, if we're able to take risks, how we receive, and ultimately, how we manifest.

Here's what I've discovered after more than two decades of walking alongside people on their healing journeys:

When we heal our relationship wounds, we don't just recover. We rise.

We unlock a kind of inner power that cannot be faked or forced. We become aligned with our true essence. Our desires become more accessible. Opportunities seem to find us easily. Dreams that once felt unreachable begin to materialize. Life starts to feel synchronistic, supported, and alive.

This is what I call "Heartbundance."

Heartbundance is more than a healing method—it's a path home to yourself. It's a method designed to help survivors of love trauma (and truly anyone who's been impacted by harmful, dismissive, or neglectful relationships) heal at the root level. It's a deep and guided process of:

- Unraveling manipulations and false beliefs we were conditioned to carry.
- Reclaiming our intuitive voice, power, and sense of worth.
- Reprogramming our self-concept to align with truth, not illusions created from past trauma.
- Restoring our innate ability to receive and manifest abundance in every area of life.

I've witnessed it again and again. A woman who spent years in emotionally abusive relationships begins to see herself clearly. And seemingly overnight, she attracts a kind, respectful partner. Another client who always felt small, muted, and invisible found the courage to step into her purpose, and her business thrived with a momentum she never imagined. One woman, after decades of surviving, people-pleasing, and self-abandoning, bought her dream beach home, and called me from the convertible she never thought she'd own, proclaiming, "I feel like I finally came back to life."

These transformations weren't because these amazing people worked harder. They happened because they were able to clear the invisible blocks that were installed by their past love trauma. They stopped believing the lies that told them they were unworthy, unlovable, or incapable. They grieved, processed, and healed. In that clearing, something miraculous happened: they became powerful, magnetic creators.

That's the essence of Heartbundance.

It's not about pretending the pain didn't happen. It's not about rushing past grief or skipping steps. It's about meeting the truth with compassion. It's about honoring your wounds while refusing to be defined by them. It's about rewriting the narrative, not with toxic positivity, but with radical empowerment.

This book is your companion on that sacred journey. It will guide you through:

- Understanding the wounds you carry from past relationships.
- Identifying how these wounds may still be operating in your thoughts, behaviors, and expectations.
- Healing those wounds at the emotional, energetic, and subconscious levels.
- Reclaiming your inner authority and realigning with your desires.
- Activating your ability to manifest the life you were always meant to live.

Before we go further, I want to tell you something deeply important: You are your own best guide. This book is filled with hard-earned wisdom, practical tools, and soul-led reflections, but at the end of the day, your intuition leads the way. If something doesn't resonate, trust yourself. If something feels true, lean into it. The goal of Heartbundance is to help you come back to your center and remember the Creator you've always been beneath the pain and traumatic programming.

This book is best used as an experience rather than information you gather but never turn to again. Let yourself have a conversation with it. Here are some tips to get the most out of this book:

1. **Don't compare your trauma to others.** Your pain is valid. Whether your love trauma came from overt abuse, emotional neglect, inconsistent love, or something that's hard to name, it matters. There is no trauma hierarchy here. We do not lose the right to our healing by having "less" trauma than someone else. We all deserve to feel whole. Comparing your wounds only dims your light and postpones your healing.

2. **Follow your intuition above all else.** Take what resonates and leave what doesn't. Your heart knows what's right for you. This book is not a rigid formula. It's a toolkit, a mirror, and a sacred space. Let it support you without overriding your own inner guidance or intuition. If something doesn't feel good or true, release it. You are always the authority in your life.

3. **Engage actively.** This book is not meant to be a passive read. It's a living conversation. When a concept strikes you, pause. Reflect. Journal. When there's a prompt, visualization, or practice, follow through to engage in the process. Don't skim with the promise to "do it later." Transformation happens when you show up fully for it and make a commitment.

4. **Be patient with yourself.** Healing is not a straight line. It spirals, deepens, contracts, and expands. Some days you'll feel powerful and clear. Other days, you may feel like you're going backward. That's okay. That's healing. Keep showing up with grace. I always tell my clients: Do as much as you can, as often as you can, and let that be enough. With that mentality, you will keep navigating toward where you want to be, even if sometimes you feel you're sprinting and other times you're taking a breather.

So, here we are. Ready to journey together through the terrain of trauma, relationship wounds, subconscious programming, empowerment, and manifestation. We're going to explore how your past experiences shaped your inner world, and how you can reclaim your power to shape your external world in alignment with your deepest desires.

And some reminders before we embark on this journey together: You're not broken. You're becoming. You're not too late. You're right on time. The fact that you're holding this book means your soul is ready to heal, rise, and remember its power.

This is the work. This is Heartbundance. Let's begin.

PART ONE

understanding the influence of love trauma

*The subconscious mind doesn't know
the difference between a saber-tooth tiger
and a yelling match with a partner
that could end the relationship.
It only knows the level of threat you feel.*

understanding love trauma

Before we can start the process of Heartbundance, we need to talk about what trauma itself actually is. Essentially, this process of Heartbundance is a process that takes you from active trauma that hinders your day-to-day well-being to shedding that and stepping into your inner authority and highest timeline.

So, let's get clear about what trauma is and what its impact on you is today, your starting point. The most accepted and research-backed definition of trauma is that it's not the event itself but the lasting impact it has on the individual. According to the Substance Abuse and Mental Health Services Administration (SAMHSA), trauma results from "an event, series of events, or set of circumstances that is experienced by an individual as physically or emotionally harmful or life-threatening and that has lasting adverse effects on the individual's functioning and mental, physical, social, emotional, or spiritual well-being."

The operative word here is *experienced*. Trauma isn't just about what happened. It's about what happened inside of you as a result. It's the perception of overwhelming threat combined with a sense of helplessness, powerlessness, or inability to escape. That's what creates the traumatic imprint in the nervous system.

To understand why this happens, we have to remember something vital: The brain you have today is a brain that was designed to help you survive. Not only was it designed to help you survive, but it's designed to survive the conditions and threats that faced our ancient ancestors thousands of years ago. Those wild, unpredictable conditions needed a finely tuned internal alert system to help them survive the realities of that time. And so, evolution prioritized safety, not happiness. All of this means that our neurological wiring (particularly our trauma responses) developed to keep us alive in the face of danger. Our brains are exquisitely sensitive to perceived threats, whether or not they're actually life-threatening in the modern world.

Let's walk through what this means with an example. Think of a prehistoric human walking through the forest. A rustle in the bushes could mean a predator. The amygdala, the brain's fear center, would immediately take over. That person wouldn't pause to analyze; they would instinctively react. They may run away, fight the threat, freeze in place, or fawn. Their heart would race, their adrenaline would spike, their thinking brain would go off-line and the instinctual and reactive part of their brain would be in control. Their survival instincts would take over, because in that moment, staying alive would be more important than being calm and reasonable.

This same system is still in place in our brains and bodies today. But instead of saber-tooth tigers, we're reacting to text messages, emotional abandonment, conflict, rejection, or threats to our sense of belonging. Oftentimes, the nervous system doesn't know the difference between a truly life-threatening situation and one that is threatening to our hearts or spirit. The body does not respond to facts but to the level of threat you *perceive*. And since humans are social creatures, threats to connection (especially in love relationships) can register in the body as danger.

Let's walk through what this looks like in modern times with an example that is common for many of us. Think of a person who's in a relationship where they're walking on eggshells all the time. Imagine that every time they shared something that impacted them in that relationship, their partner became angry or dismissive. Their nervous system would begin to associate authenticity with danger. Over time, that person's brain would adapt by silencing them. In response they may shrink, people-please, or disconnect as a survival strategy. As you can see from this all-too-familiar example, these patterns are not flaws. They are neurological responses designed to keep us safe.

This is the essence of love trauma. Love trauma is a specific kind of trauma that originates in the spaces where we are most open, vulnerable, and trusting. In an unhealthy environment or an abusive one, it can happen in our relationships with parents, family members, and certainly romantic partners. It includes experiences like emotional neglect, abandonment, inconsistency, betrayal, gaslighting, conditional love, or psychological manipulation. Over time, these experiences shape not only how we relate to others but also how we relate to ourselves, our dreams, our boundaries, and our sense of worthiness.

From a neuroscientific standpoint, relationships are inherently tied to survival. In ancient times, being part of a tribe wasn't just comforting. It was essential for survival. Rejection could literally mean death. While we no longer face the same physical dangers, the emotional experience of disconnection still lights up the brain's fear centers in the same way.

Our need for love and safety is primal.

So, when love harms us, especially repeatedly, the brain creates protective adaptations. Some of these adaptations can lead us to stop trusting, numb out, or become hypervigilant. We might internalize the harm and begin to believe it's our fault. We develop beliefs like "I'm unlovable," "I have to earn love," or "I shouldn't be so needy." These beliefs become neural grooves that shape our behaviors, choices, and even what we think is possible for us.

Let me show you how this works in real life.

A woman I worked with had a partner who would become hostile every time she wanted to spend time with her friends. At first, she argued with him when he was being so unreasonable. But over time, the stress and emotional fallout conditioned her nervous system to perceive social connection as dangerous. Eventually, she started saying no to her friends, not because she wanted to, but because the cost felt too high. A new neural pathway was created: stay small, stay safe, preserve the relationship. But this protective strategy came at a cost. Over time, she felt lonelier, less connected, and out of alignment with her authentic self.

This is how love trauma hijacks our lives. It wires our nervous systems to choose protection over authenticity, compliance over truth, and self-abandonment over connection. And the longer these patterns are reinforced, the deeper they go. They become the unseen scripts running the show, quietly dictating what we believe we're allowed to want, need, or become.

But here's the part I want you to take away as the most important part of this discussion: These patterns are not permanent thanks to a process called neuroplasticity. This is a term used to describe the brain's capacity to continuously rewire and change itself. It is real, and it happens from the time we are born until we take our last breath. Thanks to this process of neuroplasticity, we can change ourselves from within. With intention, practice, and support, we can unlearn the adaptations that no longer serve us. We can repattern our nervous systems to recognize safety in love, worthiness in being seen, and abundance in receiving.

This is exactly the work of Heartbundance.

> *Heartbundance begins by honoring*
> *the protective parts of you that have worked*
> *so hard to keep you safe.*

It helps you identify the love wounds that created the trauma patterning and gently clear them at the emotional, energetic, and subconscious levels. From there, you're invited to remember your power—not as something to strive for but as something that was never truly lost. It was just buried under layers of pain, conditioning, and survival.

When we heal our love trauma, we begin to see ourselves clearly. We stop chasing relationships that echo our wounds. We stop settling for crumbs and start embodying the belief that we are worthy of the whole feast. And in that reclamation, life begins to respond differently. Love flows more freely. Creativity returns. Dreams feel accessible. Manifestation becomes magnetic.

> *If you feel that you have been stripped away from yourself*
> *due to love trauma, please know you are not broken.*

You are brilliantly adaptive. Every part of you that coped in the face of harm did so out of commitment for your survival. And every part of you continues to be capable of healing, integrating, and thriving again.

Understanding what love trauma is and how it shapes us is our permission slip to give a name to this process we know impacted us so deeply. But it's not an invitation to stay right here. Let understanding what happened to you be an asset as you journey through your healing and transmutation. Knowing how our nervous system and neuro-connections shifted us in order to survive helps us understand how to unravel out of the chains of fear and threat moving forward. Next up, we'll explore how love trauma often materializes as a trauma pattern that you may experience in your everyday life. Identifying these patterns is a foundational step to begin the process of gently and compassionately reclaiming your wholeness.

heartbundance

The pain from trauma isn't just episodic,
it's systemic. And as a result, what emerges
is not merely a set of isolated symptoms,
but something bigger that's hidden
in plain sight: a trauma pattern.

when love trauma becomes a pattern

When we speak of love trauma, it's easy to imagine one painful moment, one terrible fight, or one particularly damaging memory that replays over and over in our minds like a nightmare. But in truth, the impact of love trauma is rarely confined to a single event. It is far more expansive, deeply rooted, and more pervasive than most people realize.

What I've seen time and again in both my personal journey and in the lives of the clients I work with is that the wounds caused by love trauma often go far beyond what we consciously remember. The pain isn't just episodic, it's systemic. And as a result, what emerges is not merely a set of isolated symptoms but something bigger that's hidden in plain sight: a trauma pattern.

A trauma pattern is the mind and body's learned way of surviving pain. It's the behavioral, emotional, and cognitive loop that gets wired into your system in response to sustained threat, criticism, or emotional deprivation. This isn't just a habit. It's a pattern of behavior, a feeling, and a state of being that is your subconscious mind's attempt at adapting to discomfort and threat. And often, it begins forming long before we even realize something is wrong.

Think back to the example I shared in the last chapter, where someone began withdrawing from their loved ones because every time they spent time with others it created tension in their romantic relationship. At first, it may have felt like a small sacrifice: "I'll just cancel this one visit to avoid another argument." But over time, the repeated exposure to conflict caused the subconscious mind to adapt. To protect the relationship (and avoid emotional punishment), the person gradually isolated away from their support system altogether. What started as a situational coping mechanism eventually became a trauma pattern: avoiding connection to avoid a perceived threat.

And that's the hallmark of a trauma pattern. It persists long after the initial danger is gone. Eventually, it becomes hardwired. The brain begins to associate certain behaviors, thoughts, or feelings with pain or threat, even if those things are no longer unsafe. These patterns can remain even when someone has been out of an unhealthy relationship for many years.

This is how trauma patterns develop: A painful experience triggers an emotional reaction. That emotional reaction leads to coping behavior. And when that behavior seems to reduce the emotional pain (even if only temporarily), the brain marks it as "safe" and repeats that pattern over and over again. With time, those repeated behaviors become ingrained, forming automatic responses that operate beneath our conscious awareness.

Even after someone has left a toxic relationship, those trauma patterns can remain. They leak into everyday life. They seep into interactions with friends, in our professional lives, even interactions with strangers. They also show up in new relationships. In these new relationships, the old rules of our traumatic past may not be relevant, but the nervous system hasn't gotten the memo yet. If left untouched, these patterns can linger for years or even decades. And they shape our beliefs, reactions, and decisions in ways that feel like "just who we are." But the truth is, they're who we became in order to emotionally survive.

Just as no two relationships are the same, no two trauma patterns are exactly alike. These patterns are shaped by the relationship itself, by the person's perception of what occurred, and by the echo of older wounds that often predate the relationship altogether. Many times, these trauma patterns can stretch all the way back to childhood. **The brain is brilliant at weaving past and present together into one storyline. And when trauma repeats in different forms across time, the pattern only deepens.**

I'd like to show you an example of this so you can see how impactful it is in "real" life. I once worked with a woman who was outwardly strong, capable, and kind-hearted. But internally, she was drowning in exhaustion, guilt, and confusion. She had recently left a relationship with a man who was hypercritical, demanding, and emotionally neglectful. During their time together, he constantly dismissed her needs and expectations, ridiculed her for speaking up, and made her feel guilty anytime she expressed desires of her own.

To survive the relationship, she learned to contort herself into the shape he needed. She silenced her voice. She suppressed her truth. She gave, and gave, and gave until there was nothing left of herself but a shell. When she came to me, she was on a path to reclaim her identity but found herself stuck in the same behavioral loop: people-pleasing to the point of self-erasure.

At first, she believed this was solely the result of the toxic relationship. But as we dug deeper, we uncovered an even earlier thread: her father. A man who, though perhaps well-intentioned, was also controlling, critical, and intolerant of boundaries. From a very young age, she learned that love meant sacrifice. That being good meant being silent. That her value was determined by how well she served others.

This wasn't just a pattern born in her adult relationship. It was reinforced from childhood. And so, to truly heal, we didn't just address the recent past. We went all the way back. We revisited the little girl who learned to make herself small in order to feel safe. We gave her voice back. We helped her see that love should never require her disappearance.

This is the essence of trauma patterning: The original wound creates a coping strategy, which becomes a pattern, which then becomes your default response to the world. That is, until it's brought to light and recognized for what it is.

When there's awareness of the pattern, healing and new patterns can interrupt the cycle.

Let me share another powerful example. One of my clients, Connor, a deeply talented and ambitious man, found himself strangely paralyzed when it came to taking career risks. Despite being fully capable and intelligent, he routinely passed up promotions, turned down exciting job offers, and avoided travel opportunities that would have advanced his career. He didn't know why he was doing this. It didn't make logical sense. But emotionally, every step toward expansion felt like danger.

As we unpacked his story, we discovered a painful pattern: During their marriage, his ex-wife consistently responded to his success with jealousy, insecurity, and sabotage. Whenever he tried to grow, she would emotionally punish him. She accused him of abandoning her, belittled his dreams, and created chaos whenever he made moves toward advancement. Over time, he learned (subconsciously) that growth equaled pain. So, even after he left the relationship, the trauma pattern continued on.

It wasn't just about promotions at that point. The pattern was ignited at the thought of any kind of expansion. This included travel for leisure, new experiences, and sharing his dreams out loud. He had internalized the belief that shining his light would cost him his comfort and peace.

But once we named the trauma pattern and linked it to its source, everything changed. Connor began to untangle himself from that fear. He started dreaming again, setting goals, and pursuing them unapologetically. Within a year, he was flying across the globe for speaking engagements, doing work he loved, and embracing life on his terms, not because the fear was gone entirely but because he reclaimed the part of himself that had been held hostage by someone else's insecurities.

At this point you're probably wondering how you can untangle yourself from these trauma patterns. If you suspect you may be living in the aftermath of a trauma pattern, the first step is awareness. Begin by identifying the original love wound. What belief or behavior seems to have taken root in you as a result of past or current toxic relationship dynamics? Do you over-give? Stay small? Avoid conflict at all costs? Struggle to ask for help? Feel guilty for being happy?

Then ask yourself this: Where else is this showing up in your life? Are you playing out the same pattern in friendships, at work, in your family, or even in the way you talk to yourself?

And finally—look deeper. Was this pattern present even before your last relationship? Did your childhood teach you something about love, safety, or worthiness that made this recent dynamic feel familiar?

Because healing doesn't happen from the outside in. It happens from the root outward.

When you follow the thread from your current pain back to the original wound, you give yourself the opportunity to rewire the pattern. You teach your nervous system that it is now safe to live differently, to speak, to risk, to expand, and to even love again.

This is the sacred work of love trauma recovery. It's not about fixing yourself. You were never broken. It's about understanding yourself. Seeing the patterns not as flaws but as footprints from where you've walked. And gently, lovingly, *intentionally* choosing a new path forward.

heartbundance

*The relationships that can rupture
our sense of self, distort our ability to love
and be loved, and leave us struggling
to trust or feel safe are far more widespread
than we often recognize.*

what kind of relationship leads to love trauma?

When we talk about love trauma (those deeply imprinted emotional wounds that linger long after a relationship has ended), it's vital that we widen our lens and take a wider look at the diverse relationships that can leave such a lasting imprint. We often assume that love trauma only arises from clearly abusive relationships, where the harm is loud, the scars are visible, and the pain is universally acknowledged. But the truth is far more nuanced. The relationships that can rupture our sense of self, distort our ability to love and be loved, and leave us struggling to trust or feel safe again are far more widespread and subtle than we often recognize.

Certainly, relationships marked by emotional, physical, sexual, or financial abuse are toxic and traumatic. This is something that, by now, most people accept and understand. Abuse in any form creates deep wounds that compromise a person's emotional safety, self-worth, and future ability to engage in secure, loving bonds. We will absolutely explore the mechanisms of this kind of trauma in depth because it is urgent and important to do so.

And as important as that is, what I also want to emphasize is that love trauma doesn't only grow from what we can clearly define as abuse. It also takes root in the quieter, yet still insidious relationship dynamics. The ones that don't scream harm but whisper it over time. The ones where there's no bruising, but there is emotional erosion. The ones that are not easily called out because they're not so easily named.

Some of the most profound emotional injuries come from relationships that look fine on the outside. Relationships where no one raised their voice or laid a hand in anger, but where one partner slowly shrank themselves to maintain the connection. Where someone had to swallow their truth, contort their identity, or suppress their needs just to preserve peace or feel a semblance of love. These are relationships shaped by emotional neglect, passive-aggressive behavior, conditional affection, gaslighting, codependency, enmeshment, or subtle control.

And because these dynamics don't match the typical image of abuse, many survivors of such relationships don't even realize they've experienced trauma. They may walk away from the relationship confused, anxious, drained, or numb. They're often struggling to trust their instincts, feeling unsure whether they're "just being dramatic," or wondering why they can't seem to move on. They may not have the language to explain what happened, not even to themselves. But the effects are real.

Let me be very clear here: **Just because something wasn't *obviously* abusive doesn't mean it wasn't deeply harmful.** Just because someone didn't *intend* to hurt you doesn't mean the relationship didn't leave wounds.

To help make sense of this spectrum of experiences, I've created a visual that I call the **Toxic Relationship Quadrant**. It maps the landscape of harm across two axes:

- **Intent to Harm** (ranging from low to high)
- **Harmful Behavior** (ranging from low to high)

These two dimensions intersect to form four distinct quadrants. Each one represents a different type of relational experience and can help you identify the dynamics you may have encountered.

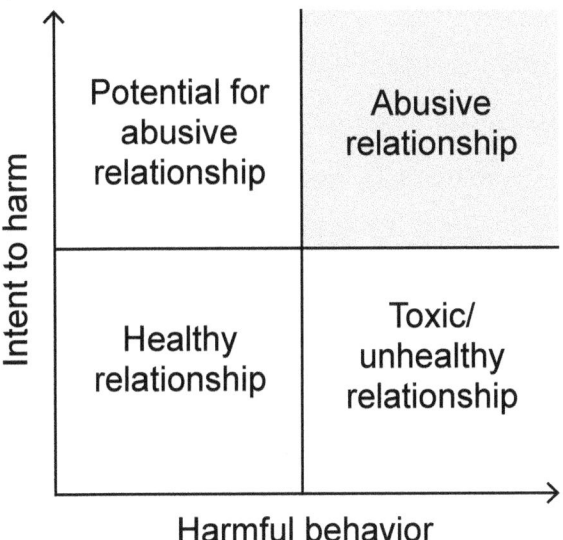

1. High Intent to Harm + High Harmful Behavior
(*Top Right: Abusive Relationship Dynamics*)

This is the most widely recognized form of toxic relationship—what we traditionally define as abuse. Here, one or both individuals deliberately engage in behaviors designed to control, manipulate, hurt, or diminish the other. The harmful actions are overt, persistent, and intentional. The emotional pain inflicted is not accidental, it's a tool to exert power and control.

These relationships are marked by patterns like physical violence, overt verbal degradation, coercive control, threats, and calculated cruelty. They often follow a cycle of tension, explosion, and reconciliation (sometimes called the abuse cycle or trauma bond), and they leave visible scars on the survivor's psyche. While the pain is obvious, the survivor's healing journey can still be complex and long. Recognition is only the first step.

2. Low Intent to Harm + High Harmful Behavior
(*Bottom Right: "Quietly" Toxic Relationship Dynamics*)

This quadrant represents relationships where the behavior is harmful (even deeply wounding) but there is little or no conscious desire to cause harm. These relationships are often characterized by unhealed wounds, inherited dysfunction, unconscious codependency, or emotional immaturity.

Partners in these relationships may truly care about each other yet still enact damaging patterns. One may silence themselves to avoid conflict. The other may avoid emotional intimacy out of fear. There may be chronic invalidation, ghosting, stonewalling, dismissiveness, or emotional inconsistency. The hurt here is not *intentionally* weaponized, but it is real. And it corrodes the self slowly, sometimes invisibly.

These relationships are particularly difficult for survivors to make sense of because there is often love present, or at least the promise of it. There may be periods of joy, laughter, and connection that seem to contradict the pain. Friends and family may not understand why the relationship left such a deep wound. And because there was no clear "bad guy," survivors often blame themselves.

3. Low Intent to Harm + Low Harmful Behavior
(*Bottom Left: Healthy Relationship Dynamics*)

This quadrant reflects a relationship grounded in mutual respect, care, and emotional safety. Conflict still happens, but it's navigated with empathy and repair. Individual autonomy is honored, and both partners feel safe to be their full selves. There is room for growth, vulnerability, and honest communication.

Even in these relationships, there may be moments of pain or misunderstanding—but they are not chronic, nor are they damaging to the core of the individual's being. Healing and safety are possible *within* the relationship, not just outside of it. This is represented on the quadrant but clearly, this relationship does not lead to the love trauma or patterning that this book aims to address.

4. High Intent to Harm + Low Harmful Behavior
(*Top Left: Grooming or Love Bombing Phase with a High Potential for Abusive Dynamics*)

This quadrant is perhaps the most deceptive. It represents the early stages of a relationship where the harmful intent to exert control or control over their partner exists, but the damaging behavior has not yet fully expressed itself. This often occurs during the grooming or love bombing phase of an abusive relationship.

At this stage, the abusive partner may appear charming, attentive, generous, and loving. But beneath the surface lies a desire to manipulate, control, or diminish the other's sense of self. The harmful behavior will increase over time. But for now, it's masked by the illusion of a new, happy relationship. When someone with the intention of power and control is in a new relationship, they often move the relationship forward quickly with love bombing and other strategies to get the person to attach to them as quickly as possible. This is why so many people don't see the red flags until they are deeply entangled.

You may find that your experience doesn't fall neatly into one category. That's okay. The lines between these quadrants are often blurred. Relationship dynamics are complex, and every person brings their own history, wounds, and patterns into them.

What matters most is not how a professional would label your experience—but how *you* experienced it.

- Did you feel emotionally unsafe?
- Did you have to suppress parts of yourself to stay connected?
- Did you walk away from the relationship feeling smaller, lost, or broken?
- Did you find yourself doubting your worth, your voice, or your right to take up space?

If the answer to any of those questions is yes, then it's worth honoring what happened. It's worth giving yourself the language to name what happened. And it is absolutely worth seeking the healing you deserve.

Whether you experienced overt abuse or subtle, soul-wearing erosion, the impact on your nervous system, your spirit, and your sense of possibility is real.

Survivors of both clearly abusive and quietly toxic relationships often carry the same core wounds: feelings of unworthiness, difficulty trusting, disconnection from themselves, and a sense of being blocked from joy or abundance.

This is not about comparison. This is about truth. And your truth is sacred.

My hope in sharing this framework with you is not to put people in boxes but to offer a compassionate map. A way for you to see yourself more clearly. A way to articulate what happened when the words were hard to find. A way to validate your experience so that the rebuilding can begin.

Because shining a light on what happened is the beginning of healing.

And from that place of truth, you can begin to reclaim your heart, your voice, your worthiness. And eventually, your power to manifest and create a future that is no longer defined by what harmed you but by what energizes you.

You can bridge a connection to find how
your love wounding may have a lasting impact
in the form of a trauma pattern. The best way to start
releasing those patterns is to bring them to light.

love wounds and their echoes

The love traumas we endure within relationships are as unique as relationships themselves. As you likely know from your own journey, no two relationships are ever the same. In fact, the only people who can truly grasp the dynamics of a relationship are the two people within it. And even then, each person likely walks away with vastly different interpretations.

That's why your love wounds, the pain you carry from the relationship, and the challenges you've faced may feel deeply personal and impossible to explain to others. Your experience is shaped by your personality, your history, your needs, your background, and by the specific relationship in which the trauma occurred. No one else has lived it like you have and can understand the impact on you the way you can.

Yet even in the uniqueness of your experience, there are threads of commonality. While every relationship is different, there are some shared emotional injuries many of us carry. These are wounds that emerge repeatedly across countless love stories turned sour. As we review these different and commonly experienced love wounds, please keep in mind that these are presented for you to compare against in order to better understand your own experience. As you read through them, think of these common wounds like mirrors. They're reflecting aspects of your experience back to you and allowing for deeper understanding.

With that in mind, let's look at what some of the more common love wounds are for survivors of love trauma together. As you read through them, please keep this in mind: This chapter is not about putting your experience in a box. It's about helping you explore from a place of compassionate reflection. As you read, allow yourself to simply notice what resonates. These categories are here to spark insight and self-awareness. They are not intended to diagnose or define you. Healing isn't about fitting into rigid definitions. True transformation begins when we come to deeply know ourselves, our pain, our patterns. From that awareness, we can intentionally choose a different way forward.

You may notice that many of these wounds overlap. That's because love trauma is often experienced as a set of overlapping experiences that bleed into one another over time. As a survivor, it's not uncommon to see pieces of your story reflected in multiple sections. Let that be okay. Let it validate, not limit, your understanding of what you went through.

My hope is that as you read through these love wounds, you find clarity regarding what happened. As you read them, consider what is part of your story. Then you'll have the opportunity to personalize and explore how this impacted you through the journal prompts. Many readers will find more than one description relatable to their experience, and there may be wounds in your story that aren't listed here. Ultimately, our goal right now is to provide you information pulled from collective experience to gain clarity. And as we do that, we can help bridge a connection to find how your own wounding may have a lasting impact in the form of a trauma pattern that you continue to carry. The best way to release those patterns is to bring them to light.

With that in mind, let's begin exploring these wounds together.

Love Wound: Being Isolated from Loved Ones

One of the most common love wounds occurs when you are slowly, sometimes imperceptibly, separated from the people who care about you. Usually, this is your family, your friends, and your support system. This can happen with obvious malicious intent, or it can happen subtly through the insecurities of a partner who feels threatened by your connection to others.

Regardless of the reason, the impact is the same: You're left feeling alone, disoriented, and more reliant on the relationship than is healthy or safe. Over time, this forced separation can plant seeds of false belief. Some survivors of this love wound feel that they're unlovable to others, that they are a burden, or that their partner is the only person who truly understands them. Those are illusions. They are not truths, but they feel real when you've been emotionally cut off from your community. The echoes of this type of love wound are feeling that it's dangerous to have a lot of vulnerable relationships, and you shrink back your connection either consciously or unconsciously. Other echoes are lacking a sense of community and support, feeling that your world has shrunk considerably, and having a heightened comfortability with codependency than is healthy. If this resonates for you and your experiences, take a look at the following journal prompts.

JOURNAL PROMPTS:

- Were you isolated from others in your past relationships?
- Do you believe it was done with intention, or out of your partner's own woundedness?
- What beliefs about yourself did you adopt during that period of isolation?
- Which of those beliefs still linger? Begin to name them as illusions—false messages born from trauma, not reflections of your truth.
- What is a small micro step you are willing to take to engage in a sense of community again?

Love Wound: Dimming Your Light in Service of the Relationship

One of the most painful and silent traumas is having to dim your light, your brilliance, your ambition, your joy, for the sake of preserving a relationship. This can happen in emotionally abusive dynamics where your growth is seen as a threat rather than something to be celebrated. Instead of encouraging you to shine, your partner may have punished you. This often happens through put-downs, resentment, silent treatment, or other subtle (or overtly abusive) forms of sabotage.

Sometimes, this dynamic also arises in relationships with insecure partners who, though not intentionally harmful, feel destabilized by your happiness or success. Their discomfort becomes a weight you carry. You learn, unconsciously, to shrink yourself so they can feel okay. Partners in this dynamic might sacrifice their joy to avoid rocking the boat. But at what cost?

This internal rewiring can cause you to fear your own greatness. It teaches your nervous system to associate success with loss, threat, or punishment, and that's a trauma worth healing. The echoes of this love wound are mighty in relation to what you step into and risks you do or do not take. It pairs visibility with threat. It leads people to question their gifts and scale back in sharing them instead of sharing them freely and openly with the world. It makes attention to their abilities and strengths feel like a threat rather than a compliment. If this is a part of your love trauma past, consider the following journal prompts for your personal discovery.

JOURNAL PROMPTS:

- How did your partner react when you felt confident, successful, or joyful?
- How do you feel now when you pursue personal growth or accomplishment?
- What physical or emotional signs tell you that your body is interpreting your success as a threat?
- What would you share with the world if you were not held back by the echoes of this love wound anymore?

Love Wound: The Highly Critical Partner

A relationship with a highly critical partner can slowly erode your sense of self. Whether they focused on your appearance, intelligence, choices, or your very essence, the constant barrage of criticism often becomes internalized. Over time, their voice becomes your inner voice. Their judgments become the story you tell yourself.

It's important to understand that while there may be reasons behind their behavior (such as their own trauma, insecurity, or even mental health challenges of their own), those reasons do not justify the harm. Your healing doesn't require that you understand their motivations. What matters most is recognizing the impact on you.

When someone constantly critiques you, the repetition creates neurological grooves. Even if your rational mind knows their words are false, your emotional brain begins to treat them as truth. That's why recovering from this love wound requires reprogramming how you speak to yourself, how you see yourself, and how you affirm your worth.

The echoes of this love wound are very detrimental. It leads survivors to struggle with their self-esteem, with their own worthiness, and with the feeling that they are capable of achieving what they truly want for themselves. It leads survivors to question everything about themselves and to have to deal with the repetitive negative feedback from the partner or family member that has now started to be perceived as their own voice. It's important to note that perpetrators of this type of love wound are often responding to their own anxiety and fears. It's important to take note of the more frequent criticisms because they usually indicate how that person felt about themselves or indicate how they wanted their partner to see themselves. If this love wound is part of your emotional abuse journey, follow these prompts to explore what this means for you to start moving forward.

JOURNAL PROMPTS:

- What criticisms did you hear most often from your partner?
- How have those words echoed in your own self-talk?
- Imagine yourself five years from now—free of those criticisms. Who are you? How do you feel?

Love Wound: Lost Identity

In some relationships, the need to maintain closeness becomes so extreme that you begin to lose your sense of self. You become enmeshed. You start morphing into the version of yourself that feels safest for the relationship, and this is often at the cost of your own authenticity and autonomy.

This kind of dynamic can look romantic on the surface: always together, sharing everything, finishing each other's sentences. But when there's no room for individuality, it becomes stifling. You stop exploring who you are. You forget your preferences, passions, or purpose. You exist in someone else's orbit, disconnected from your own center. The lasting echo of this love wound is feeling like you don't know who you are outside of a relationship with someone else, whether that's a romantic partner, a family member, or a friend with whom you develop an enmeshed relationship. It makes codependency feel normal and healthy boundaries feel like distance. It can lead survivors to be overly hypervigilant of the needs of others and ignore the internal cues and needs that they have for themselves.

If this wound resonates with you, know that reclaiming your identity is not just possible—it's a sacred part of your healing journey.

JOURNAL PROMPTS:

- How did you lose parts of yourself in the relationship?
- What traits did you develop to survive or adapt?
- What would it feel like to start over with a blank slate, exploring who you really are without the constraints of past roles?
- What parts of you are asking to be reclaimed?

Love Wound: Curated Dependence

Some love wounds are carefully crafted over time, creating a false sense of dependence that leaves you feeling trapped. This can look like financial control, emotional manipulation, or relocation away from all support systems. It might have been masked as love or care, but over time, it became clear: The dynamic was about power.

Curated dependence is an insidious form of emotional abuse because it convinces you that you can't survive on your own. But here's the truth: You can. You always could. You were simply led to believe otherwise because that made that other person feel more comfortable.

Whether this dependence showed up through financial restrictions, emotional isolation, or losing your sense of agency, the path forward involves reclaiming that power—one micro step at a time. The echoes of this love wound are deep feelings of inadequacy, uncertainty, and feeling like you "lost yourself" in the relationship. If this feels relevant to your love trauma, follow these journal prompts to start your journey back to yourself.

JOURNAL PROMPTS:

- What relationship dynamics fostered your dependence on your partner?
- What beliefs did you adopt about your ability to take care of yourself?
- Name one small doable step you can take this week to strengthen your self-trust and self-sufficiency.

Love Wound: Love as Earned, Not Given

In this type of relationship, love wasn't freely offered. It had to be earned. Oftentimes, it is "earned" through over-functioning, perfectionism, caretaking, or emotional labor. Survivors of this type of love wound usually spin their wheels and try many strategies to secure connection with their partner. For some, affection only came when they were compliant, impressive, or giving enough of themselves. This type of wound is characterized not only by emotional distance but by a feeling of not-enoughness that is the foundational reason for the distance.

There are many echoes of this love wound. Often, survivors report feeling unworthy unless they are achieving or giving. There are often vulnerability blocks, and they experience discomfort receiving love even though they crave it so much. This is often normalized for survivors, and sometimes they experience a pattern of attracting partners who take more than they give. If this resonates with you and your own past, here are some journal prompts to start healing the part of you that wanted recognition and acceptance as you are.

JOURNAL PROMPTS:

- What do you believe you had to do or be to receive love?
- Where do you still equate worth with performance?
- What would it look like to allow love in, without earning it?

Love Wound: The On-Again, Off-Again Roller Coaster

This love wound can be characterized by the trauma of emotional whiplash. It looks like being pulled in and pushed away over and over again. One moment you're everything, the next you're nothing. If this is a part of your love trauma, these unpredictable cycles may have conditioned your nervous system to live in hypervigilance, always bracing for the next emotional withdrawal or sudden reconnection.

It's easy to see how harmful an on-again, off-again relationship would be. There are many echoes of this love wound that linger such as craving intensity over consistency, confusing chaos with chemistry, feeling addicted to emotional highs and lows, or becoming afraid of stable love because it feels unfamiliar. Often, survivors of this type of love wound long for a calm, stable relationship but feel uneasy when the possibility of one is presented to them. They started to wire love and uncertain intensity together and may have to break that connection in order to clear the way for that steady, reliable relationship they truly desire. If this resonates with you, here are your journal prompts to start exploring this.

JOURNAL PROMPTS:

- What patterns of "hot and cold" existed in your past relationship?
- How did those cycles affect your sense of emotional safety?
- What would it feel like to experience calm, steady love?

Love Wound: Emotional Starvation

This love wound is self-explanatory. Essentially, your emotional needs are disregarded or outright neglected. Survivors of this love wound feel emotionally famished in the relationship. If this is a part of your love trauma, you may have asked for connection, communication, and tenderness. But instead of getting any of those requests met, you may have been met with coldness, avoidance, or neglect. Over time, you stopped asking. You learned to suppress your needs, or even felt ashamed of them.

The impact of this is mighty. It feels like you were too much or were too "needy" in the relationships. More echoes like this persist such as suppressing emotions in order to avoid future rejection, or feeling unworthy of intimacy with others in general. People who experienced this type of love wound (especially if they were emotionally neglected in their younger years by their parents) often seek emotionally unavailable partners because it feels familiar and safe to them. Even though it actually hurts. If you feel that emotional starvation is a part of your recovery story, here are some journal prompts to start exploring.

JOURNAL PROMPTS:

- When did you feel most unseen or emotionally neglected?
- What emotions did you learn to hide?
- What needs are you now willing to honor without apology?

Love Wound: Walking on Eggshells

This love wound is directly related to being with a reactive partner. You never knew what would set them off. You became hyperaware of their moods, needs, and reactions. You became small to keep the peace. Over time, your nervous system learned that love equals unpredictability and fear. This is a love wound that can happen in an overtly abusive relationship, but sometimes this dynamic happens in a quietly toxic one as well wherein the reactive partner does not have intention of hurting the other person. Even though I've repeated this before, it's worth noting again that the underlying reason for this behavior matters much less than the impact on the person harmed by it. No rationale or explanation can make this okay, and survivors deserve to focus on their own overcoming of this as opposed to why their partner did this to them.

It's not hard to imagine how difficult this can be for a survivor to heal from. There is a lot of programming from the fear and threat elicited in this type of relationship. That fear and threat probably created programming that leads the survivor to engage in a high level of people-pleasing that focuses on others' needs over their own. They may experience a fear of conflict and have difficulty advocating or speaking up for themselves. They may be more likely to stay silent to avoid tension, or feel that they're "always on edge" even when everything is calm and safe. If this is a part of your story, follow these journal prompts to help begin your healing process.

JOURNAL PROMPTS:

- How did you silence or shrink yourself to avoid conflict?
- What role did fear play in how you showed up?
- What does emotional safety mean to you now?

Love Wound: Betrayal and Broken Trust

This is an obvious love wound, but as obvious as it is, it needs to be represented here because it's so prevalent and so hurtful for survivors of this experience. When someone has been betrayed and misled in their relationship, whether through lies, cheating, or deep emotional dishonesty, their sense of trust is shattered. It's extremely disorienting when someone we love, trust, and are committed to makes the choice to deceive us. If this happened to you, you may have questioned everything about yourself in the relationship as a reaction to this trauma, including your own worth, your intuition, or even your ability to ever trust another person in a relationship again.

All those reactions to the betrayal become the echoes of this love wound. Survivors face an insidious fear of betrayal, hypervigilance, mistrust, or suspiciousness in safe relationships, or the need for excessive reassurance to feel secure. If this is a part of your own journey, here are your journal prompts to begin your recovery.

JOURNAL PROMPTS:

- How did betrayal impact the way you view trust and safety?
- Where have you internalized their actions as a reflection of you?
- What does rebuilding self-trust look like for you?

This chapter may have been extremely difficult to read. But I hope that reading through it helps you see yourself more accurately and more compassionately. The idea is not to itemize everything that happened for safekeeping but instead to name it and see it clearly as the steps to transmuting the echoes that exist from it in your life today.

***Understanding the wounding that occurred,
and becoming aware of how it constricts you
in the present, is a superpower.***

Your awareness is the foundation of interrupting your patterns from the love wounds and, over time, transmuting into the version of you that does not experience those insidious echoes anymore.

heartbundance

No matter how deep your love wounds run, no matter how long you've been repeating patterns that feel impossible to break, you can retrain your mind. You can rewire your inner world. You can, literally and figuratively, become someone new.

rewiring love trauma through neuroplasticity

There is something beautiful, almost poetic, about the fact that the same brain that was shaped by trauma also holds the key to your transformation. As you embark on this sacred journey of healing your love wounds and reclaiming the life and love you were always worthy of, it becomes essential to understand one of your greatest inner allies: *neuroplasticity.*

Neuroplasticity is the brain's innate ability to change, reorganize, and form new neural connections over time. It's the science of transformation. And it's not just a clinical term. It's a whisper of hope from your actual neurology. It means you're not stuck. **No matter how deeply your love wounds run, no matter how long you've been repeating patterns that feel impossible to break—you can *retrain* your mind.** You can *rewire* your inner world. You can, literally and figuratively, become someone new.

Imagine your mind as a vast field of soil. Every experience you've ever had is a seed. The more often something happens (especially something emotionally intense), the more that seed is watered. Over time, it grows roots and becomes a pathway. If you were in a relationship where criticism, manipulation, neglect, or control were the norm, then the seeds of "I am not enough," "I am unsafe," or "I can't trust myself" may have grown into thick vines that now obscure your vision and choke your sense of possibility.

This isn't your fault. It's your brain doing what it was designed to do, which is to *protect you* through adaptation. But here's the downside of neuroplasticity that helps you survive love trauma: What once helped you survive may now be holding you back.

Let's break it down.

If you were repeatedly punished, rejected, or dismissed for showing confidence, ambition, or vulnerability, your brain likely learned to pair those qualities with pain. Going for a promotion, expressing your needs, or stepping into your power may now be wired to feel like danger. This may persist even when, in your current reality, it's not dangerous anymore. That danger is not logical. It's biological. It lives in the deepest parts of your nervous system, where survival programming runs the show.

This is neuroplasticity in action. Not as a villain but as a misunderstood protector.

Here's the good news: Neuroplasticity isn't inherently negative or positive. It's neutral. Like fire, it can warm your home or burn it down. It all depends on how it's used.

Similar to your nervous system in general, your brain doesn't care whether a pattern makes you happy or fulfilled. It cares whether it keeps you alive. It learns through repetition and emotional intensity.

Your brain, and the connections you create in it, will default to what you've experienced the most. That's why old stories and patterns can feel so "automatic." They are. The neural pathways are already paved and well-traveled.

But this miraculous system doesn't stop evolving. You can teach your brain new associations. You can form new emotional truths. You can create new pathways, new stories, and live them.

In my work with clients, one of the first things we do is begin to map out what I call their "neuroplasticity landscape." We trace the terrain of their love history: What were they taught love was? What were they repeatedly exposed to? Were they silenced, diminished, celebrated, manipulated, cherished, or some mix of it all?

Similar to our discussion of love wounds, we also explore the echoes of those experiences. What do they believe about themselves today? What do they fear? What do they avoid? What do they subconsciously feel is "unsafe," even if their rational mind knows better?

We explore all these intricacies of their beliefs and perceptions because these internal maps are not just theories. They are *felt realities*, and the invisible blueprints by which we live.

Now it's time for you to begin tracing your own map.

Self-Inquiry: Mapping Your Neuroplasticity

Use the following journaling prompts as a guide to explore how your brain may have been shaped by your past and how you can start reshaping it.

Current Wiring (Because of My Past)	Empowered Rewiring (How I Want to Be)
This is how I currently see myself . . .	*This is how I want to see myself . . .*
These situations feel dangerous to me now . . .	*This is how I want to feel in those situations . . .*

Here are deeper prompts to support you:

- What type of relationship did I experience that contributed to my love trauma? Was it overtly abusive or more subtly, persistently harmful?

- What behaviors or traits of mine were punished, criticized, or discouraged in that relationship?

- What beliefs did I form about myself through repeated exposure to those dynamics?

- What do I now avoid, even though it could bring me joy or growth, because it feels unsafe?

- What false identities have I adopted in order to survive love trauma? And what identity would I like to begin creating now?

From Wiring to Rewiring: The New Path Forward

Remember, the brain rewires through new experiences, new evidence, and repetition. Just as repeated harm created those old pathways, repeated healing, safety, and expansion can forge new ones.

Here's how:

- **Safe Exposure**: Gently begin doing the things that your brain has labeled as dangerous but that you know, deep down, are aligned with your truth. Start small. Celebrate every step.

- **Embodied Practice**: Pair emotional safety with new action. For example, if you're afraid to speak up, practice doing it in a safe space first—like a journal, or with a therapist.
- **Inner Dialogue**: When old fear patterns arise, speak to them with compassion. "Thank you for trying to protect me. But we're safe now. We're doing something new."
- **Visual Rehearsal**: Imagine yourself in the new reality you want. Feel it, breathe it, make it real in your body. The brain doesn't distinguish between real and vividly imagined experiences—it just learns.
- **Consistency Over Intensity**: Rewiring is a marathon, not a sprint. It's not about one massive breakthrough—it's about small, consistent steps toward a new way of being.

This is a sacred invitation.

Neuroplasticity is not just science. It is sacred biology. It's the way your body and spirit conspire to give you a second chance, again and again. Yes, your brain may have once learned to protect you through withdrawal, people-pleasing, shrinking, or self-sabotage. But now, it's your time to teach it something new.

You are not broken. You are becoming.
You are not damaged. You are rewiring.
You are not your past patterns.
You are the conscious author of your next chapter.

And the story you're writing now (of power, freedom, abundance, and love) will not only reshape your brain but your entire reality.

Our earliest relationships teach us what to expect
from love. They imprint our nervous systems,
set our internal compass, and—most importantly—
teach us how much closeness, care, and tenderness
we believe we're allowed to receive.

the roots beneath the wound

In all my years of supporting people through love trauma, I can count on one hand the number of clients who didn't have early experiences that set the stage for what came later. While there are certainly cases where love trauma arises unexpectedly, and where the heart is shattered without a traceable root, those are rare. Often, the pain of a traumatic relationship echoes an earlier wound, a whisper from childhood that quietly shaped how beliefs about love, worthiness, and connection were materialized.

The truth is, our earliest relationships teach us what to expect from love. They imprint our nervous systems, set our internal compass, and—most importantly—teach us how much closeness, care, and tenderness we believe we're allowed to receive.

So, if you've found yourself in the aftermath of a painful or even abusive romantic relationship, I lovingly encourage you to consider: *What came before it?* What was love like when you were small, impressionable, and still figuring out what safety and affection felt like?

This is not meant to blame. And certainly not to overanalyze either. But to truly understand. Because if there is a root under there, healing has a better chance when we go all the way back to it.

Let's look at some of the most common early childhood experiences that often lay the groundwork for love trauma in adulthood. These aren't guarantees. They aren't prophecies. But they *are* patterns I've seen again and again in the lives of people who later found themselves hurt, confused, or stuck in cycles of emotional pain in their relationships.

1. Emotional Neglect and the Birth of Hyper-Independence

Perhaps the most widespread childhood love wound of all is emotional neglect. This doesn't mean you were physically abandoned or overtly mistreated. It means your emotional world wasn't seen, mirrored, or nurtured.

You might have grown up in a home where:

- Emotions were dismissed, minimized, or ridiculed.
- You were told to "toughen up" or "stop being dramatic" when you cried.
- Your parents were emotionally unavailable: too stressed, self-absorbed, or unaware to offer comfort.
- There was no safe space to turn to with your fears, needs, or tender feelings.

The result? As an adult, you may have a high tolerance for feeling unseen or unsupported in relationships, and not even notice it. You may pride yourself on being "strong," "low maintenance," or "independent." You meet your own needs without even realizing you have needs. You might find yourself attracted to partners who are emotionally distant because some part of you is used to that and doesn't recognize it as a warning sign.

EXAMPLE:

> Nina, one of my clients, grew up in a household where no one talked about feelings. Her father was stoic and rarely home; her mother was anxious and overwhelmed. When Nina was sad, she was told, "You're too sensitive." Later in life, she dated someone who never asked how she was doing emotionally. At first, she didn't mind. Because she didn't expect that from anyone. It wasn't until she began therapy that she realized she hadn't felt truly emotionally seen her entire life.

2. Growing Up with Critical Parents

Another common root of love trauma is a highly critical parent. If you were raised by a parent who was excessively critical, you may have internalized the belief that love is something you have to earn, prove, or work hard for. You may even believe that you're never quite good enough to receive it.

Criticism might have looked like:

- Constant correction or nitpicking.
- Being compared to siblings or others in a negative light.
- Rare or no acknowledgment of your efforts or successes.
- Feeling like you were walking on eggshells, and constantly trying not to mess up.

In adulthood, you might find yourself in a relationship with someone who is controlling, demeaning, or harsh, and it doesn't initially raise red flags. It feels familiar. You might even mistake it for passion or care.

EXAMPLE:

> Marcus always felt like nothing he did was good enough for his father, who constantly reminded him of his shortcomings. As an adult, he dated a partner who belittled his ideas and made him feel small. He stayed, thinking that if he just tried harder, he could finally "earn" love. That core wound—*I must be perfect to be loved*—was driving the show. When he saw the parallel between his father and his current partner, he was finally able to start breaking the link between needing to change or be perfect in order to finally receive the love and affection he deserved all along.

3. The Parentified Child: Becoming the Caretaker too Soon

Some children are forced to grow up far too early. If you were put in a position where your parents leaned on you for emotional support, confided in you about their problems, or expected you to act like another adult, you were *parentified*.

You may have experienced:

- Being the "therapist" for your mother or father during their own struggles.
- Being told too much about adult issues (money, relationships, etc.).
- Feeling responsible for your parent's happiness or well-being.
- Taking care of siblings while still a child yourself.

Parentified children often grow up to be caregivers in their romantic relationships. They may be challenged by patterns of over-functioning, people-pleasing, and sacrificing their own needs to keep the peace.

They struggle to ask for help. They sometimes tend to mistake over-responsibility for love.

EXAMPLE:

Jasmine's mother confided in her about everything: her failed relationships, her financial struggles, even her sex life. Jasmine felt responsible for her mom's emotional well-being. In adulthood, she dated partners who were emotionally unstable, and she always tried to "fix" them. She didn't know how to stop, and she felt she was abandoning people around her if she set limits and boundaries with them. Her nervous system was wired for over-functioning until she started to see this bridge and help herself create her own sovereignty and peace.

4. Witnessing Chaos: Normalizing the Storm

If you grew up in a home filled with yelling, unpredictability, or emotionally volatile relationships, you may have developed a strange comfort with chaos.

This can happen when:

- Your parents constantly fought or had a dramatic on-again/off-again dynamic.
- One or both parents had addictions or untreated mental health issues.
- Your emotional environment was inconsistent: one day warm, the next cold.

As a result, you may find calm, steady love "boring." You may crave intensity, drama, and passion, even when it's toxic. You may find yourself in a hot-and-cold relationship and not even realize how chaotic it is because this dynamic was normalized for you during those early years.

EXAMPLE:

> Eli's parents screamed at each other nearly every night, only to make up dramatically the next day. As an adult, he found himself in relationships with partners who were explosive, then apologetic. The push-pull felt like love. Stability made him uncomfortable. It took deep inner work to realize that peace wasn't the same thing as boredom.

If you recognize yourself in any of these early patterns, I want you to know: *It's not your fault.* You did not choose this wiring. But you *can* choose to rewire. That's the gift of healing, and that's the power of self-awareness.

If you've only been trying to heal the *latest* love trauma (without exploring what came before it), it might feel like nothing sticks. That's because the root is still alive. And to truly reroute your experience of love and create the relationship (and life) you desire, you have to go back and nurture the inner child who learned the wrong lessons about what love is and what it costs.

This is the sacred work of healing love trauma at the root.

Practices for Reconnecting with the Root

If this chapter resonates, here are a few gentle but powerful ways to begin healing from the ground up:

1. WRITE A LETTER TO YOUR INNER CHILD

Speak directly to the younger version of you who experienced emotional neglect, criticism, chaos, or adultification. Tell them what happened wasn't fair. Reassure them that it wasn't their fault. Let them know what kind of love they *deserve* to receive.

2. VISUALIZE A CONVERSATION

Imagine yourself sitting with your inner child. Ask them what they need. Listen. Speak gently. Let them feel seen. This isn't just imagination; this is nervous-system healing.

3. RECALIBRATE YOUR INNER COMPASS

Reflect on the following:

- What did I learn about love from my early caregivers?
- How might that be influencing my adult relationships?
- What kind of love feels unfamiliar but healthy?
- What kind of love feels familiar but might be unhealthy?

4. SEEK A SAFE HEALING CONTAINER

If these childhood wounds are deep (and they often are) consider working with a trained therapist or trauma-informed coach. You don't have to walk through this alone. When you are wounded in a relationship, healing in a safe relationship can be one of the most powerful medicines.

If this is part of your story, don't just pull weeds. Plant new roots. Go back with compassion, not shame. Go back with intention, not judgment. Because the way out of trauma isn't just forward, it's *inward*.

You are not doomed to repeat what was modeled. You are not sentenced to endure what you once survived. Your nervous system can learn a new language.

Your heart can remember what it always knew: that love is supposed to be safe, tender, consistent, and mutual.

And you, every single part of you, including the child within, deserves nothing less.

heartbundance

Manifestation is the art of alignment.
It's being in alignment with what we want,
believing in our ability to create it,
and acting in accordance with that belief consistently.
But trauma doesn't align. It contracts.

the love wound mind vs.
the manifestation mind:
why love wounds interfere with
manifesting our desires

Something profound shifts inside of us after love trauma. Not just a temporary heartbreak or a rough patch, but the kind of wounding that leaves a lasting impression. Our love wounds can carve themselves into our nervous systems, rewrite the language of our thoughts, and cloud our vision of what's possible.

After the trauma, after the heartbreak and betrayal, our trauma patterning continues. And as it continues, it's creating a new set of internal rules our mind, body, and soul begin to live by in order to avoid feeling that pain again. As I've made very clear, these patterns are meant to protect us, but they often imprison us.

This is where the paradox for creating a new life begins.

The very patterning that was created to keep us safe becomes the barrier to our most sacred desires. We find ourselves wanting love, success, connection, creativity, and abundance. But every time we inch toward it, something inside pulls the brakes. The nervous system flares. The heart races. Doubt whispers. Resistance rises. And often, we don't even realize this is happening. We simply feel stuck, confused as to why things just aren't working out, no matter how hard we try.

Manifestation, in its purest form, is not just about vision boards and affirmations. At its core, it's the art of alignment. It's *being* in alignment with what we want, *believing* in our ability to create it, and *acting* in accordance with that belief consistently, even in the face of uncertainty.

But trauma doesn't align. It contracts. It causes a kind of inward folding of the psyche, or the soul, and in our deeply held beliefs.

Imagine your inner world as a garden. Before the trauma, this garden is open, receptive, and fertile. Your ideas, desires, and goals are the seeds that can take root and grow. But after trauma, especially love trauma, thorny brambles begin to grow in this garden. The soil hardens. Certain areas become inaccessible. The seeds of desire may still be planted, but the environment is no longer conducive to growth.

This hardened ground is what I call the "love wound mind."

The love wound mind is not something to be ashamed of. It's not a failure or a weakness. In fact, it's a brilliant, adaptive response to pain. It's your inner child barricading the door after a break-in. It's your subconscious whispering, *We can't go through that again.* The trauma mind says, "Survival is more important than expansion." And in a very real way, it feels correct down in your core.

But it's also the very thing that stands between us and our dreams.

What Changes After Love Trauma?

When we've been wounded in love—especially repeatedly, or at formative stages in life—our sense of self becomes distorted. We no longer see ourselves through the lens of truth but through the lens of pain. This affects:

- **Self-worth**: We question whether we are lovable, capable, or deserving.
- **Perception of possibility**: Our world shrinks. We no longer believe certain things are available to us.
- **Risk tolerance**: We avoid doing things that could bring attention, connection, or vulnerability. Even if those are the very things we want the most.

These are not random obstacles. These are the echoes of trauma. Like an invisible forcefield, they block the actions, emotions, and even thoughts that would allow us to move toward our desires. Trauma tells us: "Don't try, trying could lead to pain." So, we don't. Or we try in small, self-sabotaging ways that ensure we won't get too close to what we really want.

If the love wound mind is the operating system of fear and survival, the manifestation mind is the operating system of trust and creation. The manifestation mind is not perfect or devoid of struggle. It doesn't live in a state of permanent euphoria. But it is *free*. Or at least free *enough*. Free enough to believe in what's possible. Free enough to act in the direction of one's desires. Free enough to align to what you want instead of what feels safe.

Let me define it clearly:

- *The manifestation mind* is a mind that can access clarity, neutrality, and inner quiet with relative ease.
- It knows how to *observe* negative thoughts without becoming them.
- It is *resilient* in the face of setbacks, not because it never feels afraid but because it knows how to return to a place of *truth* instead of the illusions subconsciously created through trauma.
- It holds space for desire without suffocating it in doubt or disbelief.

To be clear, everyone has mental chatter. Everyone gets triggered. But the difference is in the manifestation mind, you have the tools to come back to center. You're not at the mercy of your old patterning for safety and constriction anymore. You can feel the fear and do it anyway, because your belief in what's possible is stronger than the old belief that you're doomed to repeat the past or need to pull back because of fear.

It's much easier to manifest what you believe is possible. Not just in your conscious mind, but deep in the marrow of your subconscious. If the love wound mind is running the show, you may consciously want love, success, or abundance—but subconsciously believe you're not safe to have it.

And usually, the subconscious wins.

Manifestation isn't magic. It's physics of the spirit. It's energy and action working collaboratively together. It's the momentum of belief moving through aligned behaviors.

When you believe something is possible for you,
and you believe you're worthy of it,
you naturally begin to take the steps
that align with that outcome.

Even small steps count. As long as you're moving in the direction of your desires, the Universe meets you halfway. It's a kind of spiritual inertia: Consistent action builds belief, and belief fuels more action. This is the rhythm of manifestation.

But when the love wound mind is active, even considering those first steps can feel like standing on the edge of a cliff. To move forward feels unsafe. Your nervous system goes into fight, flight, freeze, or fawn. This does not happen because you're weak but because your body still thinks it's protecting you from a past circumstance that isn't relevant for you *today*.

And in this way, healing the love wound mind is a powerful manifestation practice. This is why healing is not separate from manifestation. It *is* manifestation.

Each time you calm your nervous system, you reclaim energy that was previously stuck in survival mode. Each time you rewrite a self-limiting belief, you create space for a new possibility. Each time you take an aligned action despite your fear, you tell your brain: "It's safe to grow now."

So, if you've been stuck, it's not because you're lazy. It's not because you're doing it wrong. It's because your love wound mind is louder than your manifestation mind right now. That's okay, and that's not your fault. But it *is* your responsibility to heal it if you want to create the life you truly desire.

Your manifestation ability isn't broken. You're just patterned away from it right now. And the good news is that patterns can be rewired.

Healing the love wound mind doesn't happen overnight. But every gentle shift matters. Every choice to soothe instead of spiral, to believe instead of doubt, to act instead of freeze are important actions toward building your bridge from survival to creation.

And on the other side of that bridge is everything you've ever dreamed of.

For now, we're going to turn our attention to how to heal love trauma and fundamentally move from the love wound mind into the manifestation mind. Healing and transmuting out of the neurological patterns that were created to keep you safe is not only foundational but also necessary to access the manifestation mind when the time is right.

PART TWO

how to heal and release love trauma patterns

*It's doing something differently, over and over,
that transforms you. It changes the very fabric
of your nervous system and subconscious mind.
And from there, you shift.*

rewriting the pattern and the art of doing something different

You've come so far already.

You've named your love trauma. You've explored the wounds it left behind. You've traced their echoes in your thoughts, behaviors, and your body's deepest responses. And now, you're standing at a crossroads. This is a sacred moment where awareness moves into transformation. This chapter is about that pivot point: the choice to do something different. The way you do something different is to intervene on changing the trauma pattern.

Let's pause for a moment and revisit what trauma patterning really is.

Your trauma patterning is not just a set of behaviors or thoughts you engage in. It's a finely tuned machine. A series of neural connections that were reinforced again and again by repetition, often born from survival. These patterns were built when love hurt you, when your needs weren't met, when connection became dangerous, and when your nervous system learned to expect pain or disconnection instead of safety and love.

They were not mistakes. They were adaptations.

But now, those very adaptations are outdated operating systems, holding you back from the life and love you truly long for. And this is where the power of neuroplasticity comes in: Your brain's incredible, innate ability to rewire itself based on what you *do*, what you *feel*, what you *believe*, and what you *repeat*.

Think of how many times those trauma patterns were repeated. Maybe it was the way you flinched inside when someone raised their voice. Or how you braced for abandonment, even when no one was leaving. Maybe it was how you apologized for things that weren't actually your fault at all. Or how you stayed quiet, even when your soul screamed to speak. These weren't one-time responses. They were grooves carved deeply into your subconscious, like rivers shaping rock.

Every repetition taught your brain that *this* was the path to take. Over and over again.

This is what makes trauma patterning feel so automatic and unconscious. It *is* unconscious, until you begin to wake up. And that's what all the work you've done so far has been preparing you for.

Imagine your brain as a dense forest. The trauma patterns are the clear, well-traveled trails. These are the paths you've walked a thousand times. They're familiar and easy to follow, even if they always lead you to the same painful clearing.

Now, imagine standing at the start of a new path. But this one is such a new trail that it barely exists. It's covered in brush, branches, and unfamiliar terrain. It doesn't *look* like the right way. But something in you knows that this is the path toward healing.

Every time you choose to do something *different*, you take a single step down that new path. At first, it's hard. The old trail keeps calling.

You'll trip. You'll doubt yourself. Sometimes you'll wander back to the familiar pain, simply because it feels safer than the unknown. But each step you take on that new trail begins to carve it deeper into the landscape of your mind. And eventually, your brain will start to prefer this new path. And farther down the line, you may start to journey down that newer path without even thinking about it.

This is neuroplasticity in motion. This leads to actual change in your trauma patterning. Not just in your thoughts but deep in your neurological wiring.

Awareness + Choice + Repetition = Transformation

The formula for changing your patterning is not complicated, but it is sacred:

1. AWARENESS: *the noticing.*
   You observe your thoughts, your triggers, your reactions in real time. You say to yourself, "Ah, there's that old pattern again."

2. CHOICE: *the intervention.*
   You pause. You breathe. You give yourself space to choose something else. Even if it's small. Even if it's just a breath instead of a breakdown. *This* is the act of doing something different.

3. REPETITION: *the commitment.*
   You do it again. And again. And again. Not perfectly. Not effortlessly. But persistently, compassionately, and consciously.

It's doing *something different*, over and over, that transforms you. And not just intellectually but cellularly. It changes the very fabric of your nervous system and subconscious mind. And from there, your beliefs shift. Your emotional responses change. Your choices begin to reflect the person you're becoming, not the person you had to be to survive.

The Highway and the Dirt Road

Let me give you a metaphor that many of my clients have found extremely helpful in understanding this process.

Your trauma patterning is like a highway. It's smooth, direct, and you could drive it with your eyes closed. It's been driven so many times that your brain defaults to it automatically. That's how strong the imprint is. But now, you're choosing to exit that well-traveled highway.

The new behavior (the new belief, the new reaction, the new self-concept) is like a barely visible dirt road. Bumpy. Unpaved. Overgrown.

At first, it takes every ounce of focus to even find the exit. Then, you need both hands on the wheel. You're gripping tightly. You're not sure if your vehicle is meant for this road. You're hyperaware of every turn.

And yes, it feels hard to exit off a well-traveled highway onto a dirt road.

But the more you drive that dirt road, the more it starts to change. It becomes easier to find. It gets cleared. It becomes smoother. Your brain begins to map it as a viable route. One day, without even realizing it, you'll find yourself choosing that path instead of the old highway. And you'll feel the shift not just in your thoughts but in your body, your energy, your emotions, your choices, your life.

This work is sacred. And sometimes, it can be frustratingly slow.

You do not need to be perfect. You only need to be willing. Interrupting a pattern can be so frustrating that it may sometimes bring you to tears. You may falter. And in those moments of frustration, I want you to remember: It's not happening to you. It's something you are experiencing, and it's headed for your healing. You are becoming someone new.

One of the most important truths I can give you is this:

Transformation isn't about never falling back into an old pattern. It's about catching yourself in the pattern and choosing differently.

At first, that choice will take everything you have. But over time, it will take less. And then one day, it won't take effort at all. It will simply be who you are. So, this chapter, and this moment in your journey, is about integration. It's about understanding that you're not broken. You are patterned.

And patterns can be rewritten.

I'm not handing you fragmented pieces of machinery. I am handing you the full system—your nervous system, your mind, your consciousness, your will—and the permission to do something extraordinary with it.

This is how healing happens. This is how transformation takes root. This is how you become not just a survivor of love trauma but a sovereign Creator of your life.

So, take a breath. Take the next step. Take the wheel with both hands. And drive yourself home to the life you were always meant to live.

In the next chapters, we will talk about the tools in your toolbox that will be your lifelines in actually changing the patterns and creating a new beginning.

*Mindfulness is the tool that helps us notice
our patterns when they're happening.
You pause before reacting. And in that pause,
you create space for something more aligned
and authentically you.*

the healing power
of mindful awareness

When you begin the journey of healing from love trauma, and when you truly commit to shedding the chains that have bound you in cycles of heartache, self-doubt, and invisible wounds, the most transformative tool you can develop isn't complicated or fancy. It doesn't require years of training or expensive courses. It's something that, at first glance, seems almost too simple.

It's *mindful awareness.*

At its essence, mindful awareness is the gentle yet powerful act of paying attention. You pay attention to your thoughts, your feelings, your body, and your reactions. This is a different kind of attention. You pay attention to all these things as they unfold in the present moment. It's the difference between robotically rotating the old story of mindless repetition and waking up to the possibility of healing. Between being hijacked by a trauma pattern and being able to witness it as it arises, making room for something different. And yet, despite how simple it sounds, mindfulness is revolutionary. Especially for a survivor of love trauma.

But let's point out the elephant in the room. Mindfulness has become a buzzword. It's been stamped on coffee mugs, folded into yoga classes, thrown around in wellness spaces, and sold as a lifestyle brand. In some ways, that's a beautiful thing. It means the idea has gone mainstream and it's more accessible than ever before.

But in that process, its depth and purpose have often been diluted. Many people hear the word and think, "Oh, that's just breathing exercises" or "That's meditation. That's not for me."

But true mindful awareness is not just about stillness. It's not about emptying your mind or becoming superhumanly calm. It's about cultivating *presence*. It's about waking up to your experience instead of being swept along by it. **And when you've been shaped by love trauma, and your nervous system has been rewired by emotional neglect, betrayal, or manipulation, mindful awareness is nothing short of a lifeline.**

Let's paint the picture clearly: The brain loves efficiency. As you've learned by now regarding neuroplasticity, your brain adapts to your experiences over time. When you've lived in survival mode (walking on eggshells, managing emotional chaos, or bracing for the next heartbreak), your mind and body start to run on autopilot.

That autopilot becomes your baseline, and you start to react in a patterned way without realizing it. You may numb without noticing it happening. You might replay old relationship dynamics without even being conscious of it. This is how people often end up reliving their love wounds, not because they want to but because they're *not aware* it's happening.

This is why awareness is foundational. Without it, you cannot change what you can't see. Without it, healing becomes like trying to paint a masterpiece in the dark.

But with this awareness? You turn on the light.

You recognize when you're slipping into old patterns. You notice the triggers before they spiral. You pause before reacting, and in that pause, you create space for something new, something more aligned, more empowered, more authentically *you*.

To understand how mindful awareness works in daily life, let's use a metaphor.

Imagine stepping into an elevator. Back in the day, elevators often played soft background music, what some called "elevator music." Sometimes it was pleasant, smooth jazz or gentle classical music. Other times, maybe it was strange or unsettling. Now, if you're on autopilot, you step into that elevator, hear the music unconsciously, ride to your floor, and walk out. You might feel slightly different; maybe more calm, or maybe more irritated, but you wouldn't know *why*.

Let's say the music was jarring, angry, chaotic. If you weren't paying attention, you might leave that elevator feeling tense, edgy, or low. In this scenario, you might not understand why you had that sudden shift in your mood. That's what it's like to live without mindful awareness. You're absorbing the world around you. You're absorbing and mindlessly reacting to all its messages and its energy without even realizing it. You're being *affected*, but you're not *choosing*.

Now imagine the same scenario, but this time, you're mindful.

You step into the elevator and immediately notice: *This music doesn't feel good*. It's grating on your nerves. Instead of unconsciously absorbing it, you *register it*. You say to yourself, "Wow, this is not the energy I want right now."

From that space of awareness, you can *choose*. You might put in your earbuds and play something soothing. You might focus on your breath. You might even strike up a kind conversation with someone beside you.

You're still in the elevator, but your experience is radically different. Because this time, you were awake and aware. And with that wakefulness came the ability to make an impactful, helpful choice for a different experience.

When you're healing from love trauma, your patterns are like that elevator music. Subtle. Constant, and easily overlooked. But they shape your day, your mood, your actions, and your relationships.

Mindful awareness allows you to say:

- *Oh, I'm feeling really anxious right now. Where is that coming from?*
- *Wow, I'm replaying that same familiar fear of abandonment again.*
- *I'm shrinking myself in this conversation. Why?*

And most importantly:

- *I can choose something different right now.*

This isn't about perfection. It's not about being hypervigilant or micromanaging every thought. In fact, mindfulness is the opposite of control. It's presence. It's *companionship* with yourself. Think of it like being a loving witness. You're not judging. You're simply watching, noticing, caring, and intentionally responding.

You don't need a meditation cushion or a guru to begin your mindfulness practice. You don't need to "clear your mind." You simply need to *notice*.

Start with the basics:

- What am I thinking right now?
- What am I feeling in my body?
- What story is playing in my mind?
- Is this pattern familiar? Does it feel old?

You can do this while washing dishes, while scrolling social media, while lying in bed at night. It's not about removing yourself from life. It's about being more *in it*, more *with yourself*. And remember, this is not about fixing. It's about befriending.

One of the most beautiful books ever written on this practice is *The Miracle of Mindfulness* by Thich Nhat Hanh. Written in the 1970s before mindfulness was a buzzword, it offers timeless wisdom in a gentle, humble tone. Thich Nhat Hanh, a Vietnamese Buddhist monk, was speaking to a Western audience long before most of us were ready to hear what he had to say. If you're curious about developing a deeper practice, that book is a beautiful place to start.

But for now, just breathe.

Slow down.

Notice the elevator music around you. And within you.

Give yourself the sacred gift of your own attention. Your healing begins the moment you do.

JOURNAL PROMPTS FOR BUILDING YOUR AWARENESS MUSCLE:

To begin practicing mindful awareness in your daily life, reflect on the following:

- **What does autopilot feel like in your body?**
  Think of a time when you "checked out" emotionally or mentally. How did your body feel? How do you know you're disconnected?

- **What are some common triggers that seem to "hijack" your mood or responses?**
  Identify a few patterns that sneak up on you. What thoughts or sensations usually precede them?

- **What does presence feel like to you?**
  Recall a moment where you felt deeply grounded or clear. What were you doing? How did it feel?

- **What might shift in your healing journey if you started noticing more, judging less, and choosing differently?**

heartbundance

Exerting a calming influence over the whims

of your nervous system

can become your superpower.

the sacred art of soothing
your nervous system

To create real lasting change, rewire your consciousness, and transform old trauma into embodied empowerment, then you must begin with nervous-system regulation. This is not just nice-to-have. It shouldn't be treated as a luxury or something you'll get to "when things settle down." This is foundational. It is the heartbeat of healing. Without learning to soothe your nervous system, the path to rewiring your brain, changing your trauma patterns, and stepping fully into your power will remain blocked by the very trauma from which you are trying to heal.

Your nervous system is your body's surveillance and safety mechanism. It's a brilliant, ancient part of you. It's made up of your brain, spinal cord, and network of nerves, and it acts as the communication system between your body, your brain, and your heart. Its job is to keep you alive. It scans for danger, tracks safety, and decides in a nanosecond (often without your conscious permission) whether it's time to fight, flee, freeze, or fawn.

But here's where it gets tender. If you've lived through trauma (especially some type of love trauma), then your nervous system may have learned to respond to everyday experiences as though they are life-threatening. A text message from a partner, an unanswered call, a certain tone of voice, or even love itself may trigger your system into alarm. Not because something is actually wrong but because, once upon a time, something *was*.

This is the sacred wound patterning of the nervous system. And this is where exerting a calming influence over the whims of your nervous system can become your superpower.

And here is the CliffsNotes' version of why that is: If you want to change your patterns—to stop reacting in fear, spiraling into old survival responses, or pushing love away because it feels too dangerous—you must begin by shifting the signals your nervous system is sending to your brain. In short, you must *soothe the body* so the mind can rewire.

Similar to mindfulness, the phrase "soothe your nervous system" is everywhere. It's also become a hashtag and a wellness meme. But behind the buzzwords lies a deep, intimate, and embodied practice. Soothing your nervous system isn't just about feeling "calm." It's about building safety inside your body. It's about recognizing the early whispers of dysregulation *before* your system screams in panic.

It's about becoming your own first responder, and tenderly catching your internal distress signals and gently saying, "You're safe now."

Before you can soothe your nervous system, you must learn to listen to it. Everyone's distress signals look a little different. But here are some common signs of nervous system dysregulation:

- Feeling dizzy, shaky, or breathless
- Sweating or getting cold for no reason

- Wanting to run away or hide
- Feeling detached from your body or environment
- Tightness in the chest, throat, or stomach
- Racing thoughts, spiraling anxiety
- Irritability, numbness, or overwhelm

But these are the *loud* signs. The screams. Your most powerful healing will come when you start catching the *whispers*. Those are the micro-signals that come *before* escalation.

Ask yourself:

- What happens in my body just before I get overwhelmed?
- What small shift in sensation or emotion signals that I'm slipping out of safety?
- Are there certain people, places, or situations that reliably stir up anxiety—even if nothing "bad" is happening?

This level of self-awareness is not about blaming yourself.
It's about reclaiming power.

The more fluent you become in your body's language, the sooner you can intervene and the less often you'll need to rescue yourself from a full-blown spiral. Using the mindful awareness from the last chapter, you can attune to yourself in a way that you are aware of what's happening. When you're in that autopilot mode, it's hard to notice and pivot when you need to. But using mindful awareness, you can move from autopilot where you may be reacting instinctually in accordance with those trauma patterns and intentionally soothe your nervous system to begin your new pattern interruption.

With your mindful awareness, "listen" for those signs that your nervous system is getting keyed up. And when you notice that it is, let's explore what you can *do*.

You don't need a thousand techniques. You only need a few that work for *you*. Below are some of the most effective, research-supported, and deeply healing practices you can try.

1. 3:6 Breathing

Breath is one of the most powerful tools you have. When used intentionally, it sends a message directly to your brain: *We're safe now.*

The 3:6 Technique:

- Inhale through your nose for 3 counts
- Exhale through your mouth for 6 counts
- Repeat for 2–5 times

Make sure the out-breath is twice as long as the in-breath. Why? Because it recalibrates the carbon dioxide and oxygen ratio in your bloodstream, which helps interrupt panic at the physiological level.

This technique has been so effective in trauma recovery spaces that many therapists call it a "natural Xanax." It works. And the more you practice, the faster it kicks in.

2. Square Breathing

Perfect for when your mind is racing.

Square Breath Technique:

- Inhale for 4 counts
- Hold for 4

- Exhale for 4
- Hold for 4

Repeat while mentally drawing the shape of a square. This visualization anchors your focus and slows your system.

3. Distraction (Intentional, Not Avoidant)

Distraction gets a bad rep. But used intentionally, it can be lifesaving. When your thoughts are spiraling, distraction helps reroute the mental track.

Try this:

- Find a word nearby (e.g., a book title or product label).
- Spell it *backward* out loud or in your head (e.g., "volume" becomes "E-M-U-L-O-V").

This simple shift can interrupt the pattern and give your brain a chance to calm down.

You can also ground yourself in a single *indisputable fact*—something your mind won't argue with. Example: "The sky is blue." "My feet are touching the floor."

4. Body-Based Techniques

If you're more somatic in nature—meaning your anxiety shows up mostly as physical tension—try these strategies:

- **Progressive Muscle Relaxation:** Tense and release muscle groups from head to toe (or toe to head). This signals to your brain that it can let go.

- **Drop Three:** Release tension in your jaw, your shoulders, and your belly. These three areas often store trauma and stress. Letting them freely reduce tension and tightness can instantly create a sense of grounded calm.
- **Hot or Cold Therapy:** This could be in the form of a warm drink, a cool washcloth, or a warm bath. These temperature-based shifts can signal safety and presence to the nervous system.
- **Aromatherapy:** Scents like lavender, frankincense, or orange can soothe the brain's limbic system (the emotional center).

5. Connection, Co-Regulation, and Sacred Safety

Sometimes, we can't soothe ourselves alone. We need another nervous system from which to borrow. This can be a calm presence, a soothing voice, someone who looks us in the eye and says, "You're okay."

This is called co-regulation, and it's how we first learned safety as infants. It is not a weakness to need others. It's biology. Whether it's a friend, a therapist, a trusted partner, or even your pet, being in the presence of regulated, calm energy can help your own nervous system downshift into peace.

The Path of Mastery: Repetition, Repetition, Repetition

Like any skill, soothing your nervous system takes practice. At first, it may feel awkward or ineffective. But stay with it. Repetition is how new patterns form. Each time you interrupt an old trauma response with breath, with presence, or with soothing, your brain learns a new way. Your body responds to a new signal. Your soul starts to believe: *Maybe I really am safe now.*

And over time, what once triggered you will lose its charge.

Your New Superpower

Being able to self-soothe and to down-regulate your nervous system after love trauma is nothing short of a superpower. It is the most compassionate rebellion against the past. It is the moment you stop being defined by what happened *to* you and start living from the truth of who you are becoming.

You are not broken. You are rewiring. And with every deep breath, every drop of muscle tension, every whispered reminder that you are safe, you are stepping more fully into the empowered, calm, manifesting version of you that this world *so deeply needs* and that you, yourself, deserve to be.

So, keep going. Keep soothing.
Keep returning to yourself.

You are not your thoughts.
And just like any experience,
you can change how you relate to them.

changing your relationship with your thoughts

One of the most profound questions that trauma survivors ask me is this:

"How do I stop my thoughts from hijacking my life?"

This question isn't just asked by those healing from love trauma but by anyone whose nervous system has ever been shaped by pain, neglect, betrayal, or fear. The question reflects something universal. Because let's be honest; every single one of us, whether we've endured significant trauma or not, has been haunted by wild, intrusive, or disempowering thoughts.

If we could hook a megaphone up to any one of our brains and broadcast our inner monologue out loud for even ten minutes, the world might think we've all lost it. Truly. Our thoughts are chaotic, often irrational, deeply personal, and sometimes unrecognizable even to ourselves.

Yet for trauma survivors, and especially for those carrying the heavy weight of love trauma, these thoughts don't just *come and go*. They *cling*. They *loop*. They scream rather than whisper, grabbing attention like flashing neon lights in the dark. They don't just float by. It can feel like they grab you by the throat.

And many of us start to believe them.

We don't just hear the thought: "I'm not good enough," "I'm too broken," "They left because of me," or "I'll always be alone." We *merge* with the thought. We become it. And in doing so, we lose ourselves.

For many trauma survivors, thoughts become shackles. They are tight, constricting, sometimes invisible but always heavy, and we feel trapped by our own inner monologue. These thoughts dictate what we believe is possible for us. They trap us in fear, in helplessness, in a hopeless repetition of old stories that were never true to begin with. The stories aren't just about the past, they're about identity. And unless we interrupt the cycle, we keep believing the lie that says, "This is who I am."

But I want you to know something with absolute certainty: You are not your thoughts.

You experience your thoughts. They pass through you. They are part of your awareness, but they are not your truth. And just like any experience, you can change how you relate to them.

This isn't about silencing your mind through brute force. It's not about fighting every negative thought until you're exhausted. It's about learning to *watch*, to *observe*, and most importantly, to *choose* how much power you give each thought.

Let me introduce you to something I call the Waterfall Technique.

This is not just a visualization, it's a paradigm shift. A transformation in how you relate to the very mechanism of your own mind.

Imagine you're in a tropical paradise. The kind you see in movies. There's lush greenery, a soft mist in the air, and a waterfall cascading down into a serene lagoon. In nearly every one of those cinematic moments, the characters eventually go *behind* the waterfall. They discover a little cave or sanctuary tucked away behind the falling water.

Now imagine this: You are the person behind the waterfall. The water, which is endless, rushing, and constant, is your stream of consciousness. The water represents all your thoughts.

All day long, thoughts pour down like water. Some are beautiful, clear, and refreshing. Some are murky, loud, and disorienting. But none of that changes the truth:

You are not the water. You are the observer behind the falls.

When you adopt this perspective, and this identity as the observer, something miraculous happens. You create space between you and your thoughts. You begin to watch them instead of being swept away by them. You realize they are not always wise, not always kind; often, they're not even *true*.

And in this space, with this sacred distance, you gain power. You're no longer a passive recipient of your thoughts. You become the *chooser* of that with which you engage.

You might have noticed that some thoughts seem louder, more persistent, and harder to ignore.

This is because trauma wires the nervous system to be hypervigilant. It tunes your brain to look for danger, to remember pain, and to replay moments that hurt you. Because, once upon a time, your survival depended on it. The brain, in its attempt to protect you, flags those thoughts with a giant flashing sign: "Pay attention! This matters!"

But the brain is not always accurate in determining what's useful. This is why trauma-related thoughts seem to dominate our awareness. They've been neurologically tagged as important. But with neuroplasticity and awareness, you can retag them. You can demote them. You can create new tags: of peace, of neutrality, of self-trust.

I'm going to help you understand how you can begin to rewrite the narrative of your mind. But first, here's a key truth I want you to hold on to: Thoughts are experiences. They are not declarations of truth. They are not verdicts. They are not commands. They are something you witness. Not something you *are*.

When you learn to observe your thoughts like clouds in the sky, like leaves in a stream, or like water pouring down a waterfall, you no longer feel compelled to obey them. You start choosing which thoughts deserve your energy, and which don't.

This is the heart of trauma recovery: reclaiming your agency. And not just in the outer world but in your inner one too.

A Simple Practice: Observing the Waterfall

Let's try this now:

Step 1: Watch the Waterfall

- Set a timer for three to five minutes.
- Sit quietly. Close your eyes if you feel safe to do so.
- Simply observe your thoughts. Let them come and go without engaging with them.

- Imagine yourself behind a waterfall, watching the thoughts pour down in front of you.
- Notice how some thoughts call your name more loudly. Just acknowledge them, then let them pass like water.

Step 2: Name the Loops

- Write down five thoughts that you notice coming up again and again.

These might be anxious thoughts, self-critical beliefs, or worries rooted in your past love trauma.

Step 3: Support Yourself with Tools

- For each thought, choose one nervous-system regulation tool (from Chapter 12) that you can use when it shows up.

The goal is not to "fight" the thought—but to *support yourself while it passes*.

Step 4: Ask the Golden Question

- Each time you notice one of these thoughts, pause and ask:
- "If this thought were just a sound in the waterfall, would I need to engage with it?"
- "Is this thought asking for truth or safety?"
- "Is this thought rooted in my past or my present?"

Now, imagine this practice becoming a part of your daily life. Imagine yourself observing your thoughts instead of reacting to them. Imagine what it would be to support yourself instead of spiraling and interrupting anxious cycles with compassion, regulation, and awareness.

Six months from now, what would your life feel like? Compare that to a future where every intrusive thought still dictates how you feel, how you act, and what you believe. The difference is vast. The difference is freedom.

Because *you* get to choose what kind of relationship you have with your thoughts. And in that choice, you get so much authenticity and wholeness without interference from past trauma. Remember: You are not broken for having irrational and painful thoughts. You are human. And being human means learning how to navigate the direction of your mind. Let the waterfall pour. You'll be safe behind it. Watching, choosing, intentionally responding, always evolving.

JOURNAL PROMPTS TO GET STARTED:

1. What repetitive thoughts or beliefs tend to hijack my peace the most?
2. How have I historically reacted to these thoughts? What emotions do I notice when I experience them?
3. What would it look like to become the observer instead of the believer of these thoughts?
4. What nervous system tools help me return to center when a thought is overwhelming?
5. How might my life change if I practiced "watching the waterfall" for the next ninety days?

heartbundance

There is a version of yourself
that's been there all along, waiting patiently
to be unearthed beneath the trauma patterns.

rediscovering the self
beneath the wounds

There comes a sacred point in the healing journey. It often arrives quietly, and sometimes unexpectedly. This pivotal moment is when you begin to feel just a little more at home in your own body. Your breath deepens. Your thoughts slow. Your chest doesn't feel so tight. You might find yourself exhaling and realizing *you're not bracing for impact anymore.*

This is the moment when the healing you've been working toward begins to create real space inside of you. The fight-or-flight energy that once pulsed constantly in your nervous system starts to settle. And for the first time in a long time (or maybe ever), you begin to feel something remarkable:

You begin to *rediscover yourself.*

Not the version of you that was shaped to survive. Not the version of you that had to contort yourself to stay safe or accepted. But the *real* you. This is the version of you that has always been there all along, waiting patiently to be unearthed beneath the trauma patterns, the false beliefs created from past pain and programming.

This rediscovery is not a quick or linear process. It's tender, raw, and often surprising. It's the most meaningful and sacred gift that emerges when you've begun to soothe your nervous system, reclaim mastery of your thoughts, and excavate the layers of love trauma.

The You Who Remains

When you begin to release the residue of love trauma whether from betrayal, emotional abuse, neglect, manipulation, or chronic invalidation, you don't just remove pain. You also create space. And in that space, you get to meet yourself again.

Trauma often teaches us to disconnect from who we truly are. It teaches us to prioritize the needs, moods, and demands of others in order to stay safe. It teaches us to suppress our instincts, deny our desires, and question our worth. Over time, this becomes so normal that we forget we're even doing it.

So, when the noise quiets, and the anxiety softens, the intrusive thoughts slow down, and your nervous system stops screaming that you are in constant danger, you might realize:

I don't have to overlook what I want or need anymore.

And that realization is a sign that you're *ready*. You are finally safe enough, inside your own body and mind, to ask the most important questions:

- Who am I underneath the pain?
- What actually brings me joy?
- What makes me feel alive?
- What kind of love do *I* want?
- What kind of life do *I* want to create?

I remember a client—let's call her Maya—who had done deep and powerful trauma work. She went through years of emotional abuse where her every move, preference, and opinion had to be filtered through someone else's approval. Her nervous system had been trained to scan for danger, to anticipate the emotional weather of her partner, and to suppress her own truth in order to stay "safe."

By the time she came to me, she had already done the brave work of beginning to heal her trauma. But she hit a strange point in her journey. She said, "I feel better . . . but I don't know who I am anymore."

So, I told her something that made her laugh out loud: "Maybe it's time to start dating yourself."

She gave me a look. "What does that even *mean*?" she asked.

And we talked. We laughed. But slowly, seriously, we unpacked what that might look like for her. Not in some abstract spiritual sense, but in *real life*.

What if she went out to dinner on her own? Not to please someone else but just to try something new and discover what *she* liked?

What if she walked into a bookstore and picked up whatever caught *her* eye?

What if she explored a hobby that had always intrigued her but never felt "acceptable" or "practical" in her past relationship?

And she did it. Slowly, gently. At first, it felt strange. But then she started to feel energized.

She tried new foods. She danced to music she loved. She wore clothes that *she* liked. She started asking herself questions no one had asked her in years, not even herself.

What are my values now? What kind of people feel nourishing to be around? What kind of energy do I want in my relationships?

These might sound like small things, but they were *monumental*. They were her reclaiming the brush and painting her own life again.

So many survivors of love trauma were forced to shrink or shape themselves to survive. They became experts at sensing the room, reading subtle cues, anticipating others' needs, staying quiet, staying small, staying agreeable. And they may have even built entire lives around those protective identities.

But underneath all of that, you still remain. You, the sovereign self. You, with your creative force intact. You, the one who dares to feel, to choose, to *be*.

The journey back to yourself isn't always easy.
It requires courage, patience, and curiosity.

It means grieving the years you didn't get to be fully you. And it means daring to believe that you're not only allowed to be yourself now but that you are *worth knowing*.

But don't rush through your reunion with your authentic self. It's a homecoming, not a rebranding. And homecomings are often tearful, awkward, bittersweet, and beautiful all at once.

From this point forward, you don't have to become anything for anyone else.

You don't have to perform.

You just have to meet yourself again, the way you'd greet an old friend you've missed dearly. Because the real and whole you has always been waiting underneath what you survived.

And you can finally meet again.

JOURNAL PROMPTS FOR REDISCOVERING YOU:

If you're ready to begin this process, here are some gentle invitations to explore:

- What do I truly enjoy doing when no one is watching?
- What environments make my body feel relaxed, safe, and expansive?
- What dreams did I once have that I buried to survive?
- What parts of me have I hidden because they were rejected in the past?
- What do I desire more of in my life?
- What boundaries do I need to feel more like myself?
- What does authenticity feel like in my body?

Your story is never finished.
It will never be frozen in time.
It continues to evolve as you evolve, right in step with you.
And even though trauma distorted the story,
healing will reveal the truth.

rewriting your story and becoming the author of your life

One of the most powerful and transformative aspects of healing from love trauma is this: *You get to rewrite your story*. Not just in a metaphorical way, but in a deeply real, tangible, identity-shifting way.

Before we've done our trauma work (before we've healed, processed, and made sense of the pain), we often tell ourselves a version of our life story that is filtered through the lens of our wounds. That version is usually shaped by self-blame, distorted perceptions, limiting beliefs, and inherited emotional narratives from the past. We speak of what happened to us in a way that reflects the trauma, not the truth.

But when you begin to heal, something incredible begins to happen: The fog starts to lift. The confusion begins to settle. And for the first time in a long time (maybe ever), you begin to see things more clearly. You start to understand what really happened, what was yours, what wasn't, and what you deserve moving forward.

This is the journey of rewriting your story.

Before healing, most survivors of love trauma tell stories laced with shame, confusion, and hidden grief. These stories often sound like:

- *It's my fault. I picked the wrong person again.*
- *I stayed too long. I'm so stupid.*
- *Maybe if I had just loved them better, they wouldn't have treated me that way.*
- *I guess I attract broken people.*

And while these thoughts may feel like facts, they're not. They're echoes of pain. They are trauma scripts, not truths. They are the residue that remains after all the gaslighting, abandonment, emotional neglect, or manipulation.

Before trauma healing, we don't just carry wounds. We carry the stories we told ourselves about why we got hurt. And those stories can be far more damaging than the events themselves.

Healing asks us to revisit the stories we've told ourselves with gentleness, compassion, and without judgment.

Not to relive the pain but to *re-examine it with more distance and more clarity.*

Here are some questions to sit with as you begin this process:

- What do you believe happened to you?
- Who were you in that story: hero, victim, survivor, scapegoat?
- Who held the power?
- What did you believe about yourself because of what happened?
- In what ways did you carry responsibility that wasn't actually yours?
- What parts of the story feel blurry or unresolved?
- What have you been punishing yourself for all these years?

Take your time. There's no rush. This is sacred work.

One of the most common threads I see in my clients is the quiet, persistent belief that it was somehow all their fault. Let me share an example. Colleen had spent over a decade in a relationship with a man who consistently invalidated her feelings, stonewalled her, and withheld affection when she did anything that upset him. When she finally left, she said, "I guess I'm just bad at relationships. I pick the wrong people." But as she began her healing journey, Colleen began to see more clearly. She hadn't chosen someone "wrong," she chose someone who mirrored her earliest wounds. Her story wasn't about being broken or unworthy. Colleen's story was about being someone who didn't know what healthy love looked like but was brave enough to seek it now.

Another client, David, blamed himself for staying in a toxic dynamic with a controlling partner. "I should've left the first time she screamed at me," he'd say. But as David worked through his healing, he realized how shame and emotional abandonment from childhood had made him tolerate mistreatment longer than he should have. "I didn't stay because I was weak," he finally admitted. "I stayed because I didn't realize it wasn't normal."

These shifts don't happen overnight. But they are life changing.

The beauty of trauma work is that you don't have to sit down with a pen and forcibly rewrite your life's narrative. You don't need to fake empowerment. You don't need to fabricate a new perspective. The story *rewrites itself* as you heal.

The tools of revision are you soothing your nervous system. You practicing mindful awareness. You learning how to respond instead of react. You grieving your past with compassion, and you reclaiming your self-worth. Your understanding of the story changes organically and steadily as a result of all those things you put in place.

Think of it like the metaphor of a "before and after" photo. When someone's on a health journey, they might take a photo before they begin. They might appear tired, unhappy, or confused. Then, months later, they take another photo: clearer eyes, more energy, a sense of strength. There's clearly a difference, especially when you look at them side-by-side.

Your story is the same. The "before" version of you may be filled with self-blame, confusion, and emotional fog. But the "after" version? That's the story told by a person who reclaimed their power. Who sees the red flags in hindsight, not with shame but with wisdom. Who knows that they didn't "deserve" the hurt. They were simply doing the best they could with the tools they had.

In the early stages of healing, many survivors describe the aftermath of love trauma as walking through a dense emotional fog. It's hard to remember what actually happened. It's hard to trust your own memory or gut instincts. That fog is real. It's the nervous system in self-protection mode. **But just like a foggy morning gives way to sunlight, your clarity will return and give way to peace.**

So, if right now your story still feels confusing, if you still wonder whether it was "really that bad," or if you still feel like it's all your fault, just take a moment. Pause. Breathe. Give it time. You don't need to force understanding. You don't need to rush forgiveness or rewrite anything right this hot minute.

Just keep committing yourself to doing the work. And the clarity you're seeking will inevitably come.

When that clarity does arrive, here's what your new story might sound like:

- *I didn't cause the harm. I was in survival mode.*
- *I stayed because I didn't yet know how to leave. And now I do.*
- *I was manipulated into believing it was my fault. It wasn't.*
- *I didn't have the tools or support I needed, but I do now.*
- *I was never too much. I was never not enough. I was just in the wrong place.*
- *I've grown. I've healed. And I know what healthy love looks and feels like.*

That's the truth of your story. That's the story you're rewriting with your healing. Your story is never finished. It will never be frozen in time. It continues to evolve as you evolve, right in step with you. And even though trauma distorted the story, healing will reveal the truth.

You are the author now. You're not just a character in the story, you're the one writing the script and what's going to happen.

And what a powerful thing that is.

A Practice for You: Revisiting Your Story

You may wish to do this as a journal prompt or a reflection practice over time.

1. Write your "Before" story:

- How did you explain your past relationship before you began healing?
- What language did you use?
- How did you speak about yourself?
- What emotions dominated that version of the story?

2. Write what you know now:

- How do you understand what happened differently?
- What do you see more clearly?
- How do you speak to yourself now?

3. Compare with compassion:

- What has changed?
- What hasn't yet changed?
- Can you honor the version of you who wrote the first story, and celebrate the one who is writing the second?

heartbundance

You can train yourself to recognize the trauma-induced perceptions and consciously shift into a new way of seeing. It doesn't happen all at once. But like a photographer changing a lens to better capture the light, you can learn to shift perspectives.

seeing through the lens of love trauma and learning to take it off

When you've been through a traumatic love relationship (especially an emotionally or psychologically abusive one), something fundamental begins to shift within you. Not always all at once, and not always in a way you can name. But over time, your internal compass starts to get off kilter. And with it your way of interpreting life, relationships, your worth, and your capacity could get distorted.

What actually changes is your *perceptual reference point*. Think of this like the lens of a camera: Everything you see, everything you feel, and every decision you make gets filtered through it. The colors are different. The angles are skewed. The sharpness is dulled, or it's sometimes too sharp in the wrong places.

And this lens wasn't something you chose. It was built, slowly and sometimes silently, by your nervous system trying to protect you. And by your brain's attempts at adapting to survive. By the repetition of invalidation, criticism, manipulation, betrayal. By the heartbreak of being unloved in the exact place you most longed to be loved.

Let's take a moment to honor something really hard: The fact that trauma doesn't just *hurt* you—it changes the way you *see*. And it changes the way you see *yourself*.

One of the most courageous steps of the healing journey is realizing that what you believe about yourself may not actually be *your* belief. It may be the echo of someone else's cruelty, fear, or control.

Let me share a story to illustrate this. One that still stays with me.

I once worked with a woman named Alice who was one of the most naturally gifted and capable people I've ever met. She had golden hands with unique talents. She was able to craft, build, fix, and design pretty much anything. Her carpentry, her vision, her ability to solve complex structural problems with ease was nothing short of inspiring.

But when she came to me, she didn't feel that way. Not even close.

After years of being in a relationship with a partner who verbally dismantled her, piece by piece, she no longer trusted herself. He repeatedly told her she was incapable, irresponsible, and foolish. That he had to "do everything for her." And over time, this narrative took root. But not just in her mind, in her *body* too. Alice's posture changed. Her tone softened to a whisper. Her hands hesitated where they once reached out boldly.

She no longer believed she could manage projects alone. She second-guessed her skills. She felt socially clumsy in gatherings where she once felt confident. Even her role as a mother felt compromised. She felt unsure, timid, and easily flustered. The trauma had not only impacted her emotions but also infiltrated her entire sense of identity.

She was wearing the lens of her trauma. She had looked through it for so long, she didn't realize she had it on anymore. What we began to do together was name this lens. We examined the way her internal voice sounded when the lens was in place: harsh, shaming, defeated.

We tuned into what it felt like in her body. It felt like a tight chest and sluggish energy; it felt like her nervous system was on alert and she had knots in her stomach.

We tracked the moments it showed up the most. It happened a lot when she was trying something new, when others praised her, when she was stepping into her role as a mother or making a creative decision.

And slowly, gently, we began to practice *taking the lens off.*

This didn't mean denying the pain or pretending she wasn't affected. It meant learning how to recognize when the trauma lens was speaking, and when *she* was speaking. We practiced awareness. We rebuilt trust in her abilities, not just through talk but through embodiment. Letting her build, create, move, and feel her power returning.

She learned to say to herself: "This doubt I'm feeling right now isn't the truth. It's the residue of what I was taught to believe about myself."

And that changed everything.

If you take one thing from this chapter, let it be this: Your trauma lens is not the truth.

It's a filter. A distortion. A coping mechanism that once protected you but now may be limiting your growth, your self-worth, and your ability to thrive.

When you look at yourself and see "not enough," pause. Ask yourself: Is that truly me speaking? Or is that the lens I've been taught to look through?

When you're about to take a leap to start a new relationship, create something new, set boundaries, or apply for a job and you freeze in self-doubt, ask yourself: Is this hesitation mine? Or is it old programming?

Because here's the miracle of being human: You can change lenses. **You can train yourself to recognize the trauma-induced perceptions and consciously shift into a new way of seeing.** It doesn't happen all at once. But like a photographer changing a lens to better capture the light, you can learn to shift perspectives. And the image you see begins to reflect something more accurate, more loving, and more true.

In all the years I've done this work, I've never seen two trauma lenses that are exactly the same. Each survivor builds their lens based on the specific dynamics of their trauma, their personality, their past, and the stories they were told or came to believe.

Maybe your lens tells you you're too much or not enough.

Maybe your lens tells you no one will ever stay.

Maybe your lens whispers that your worth is tied to your performance, your looks, or your sacrifices.

Maybe your lens convinces you that if someone doesn't choose you, it's because you're unlovable, not because *they're* incapable of love.

So, I can't tell you exactly what your trauma lens says. But I hope this chapter helps you discover it.

A JOURNAL PRACTICE TO UNCOVER YOUR TRAUMA LENS:

Take some time with these questions. You might want to come back to them multiple times. Let them stir something deep and true within you:

- **What do you believe about yourself in your lowest moments?** Write it out. Be honest. What's the story you tell yourself when you feel rejected, unsure, vulnerable?

- **What are the words that run through your mind when you're afraid to take a risk?** Where did those words come from? Do they echo anyone you used to know?

- **How does it feel in your body when that trauma lens is activated?** Do you tense up? Go numb? Collapse inward? What does your nervous system do?

- **What happens spiritually when this lens is on?** Do you feel disconnected from your sense of purpose, intuition, or the Divine?

- **What would it mean to live without this lens?** If you could see yourself clearly and kindly, how would your life change?

- **What situations trigger the lens most strongly?** Make a list. These are your growth points. These are the invitations to awareness.

- **What would a new lens say instead?** Try writing a few new truths. Ones that feel just a little more loving, a little more real.

The hardest part of transforming the lens is learning to *notice* when the lens is on. But once you develop this skill, everything changes. You don't have to fight yourself anymore. You can simply say, "Ah, this is the lens in action," and then choose whether to keep it on or take it off.

This is not toxic positivity. It's not denial. It's choosing to tell the truth about what's true *now*, not what trauma once led you to believe.

So, here's your reminder:

> *You are not broken.*
> *You are not inadequate.*
> *You are not too much.*

You are a soul who learned to see through survival. And now you're ready to see reality as it is, unfiltered by the past.

heartbundance

Corrective experiences are so vital
because they help you disprove the illusion that trauma
hardwired into your mind and nervous system.

the power of corrective experiences

One of the most essential and empowering parts of the healing process is something I call *corrective experiences*. These are moments, opportunities, and actions that begin to restore what trauma tried to steal from you. And believe me, trauma (and especially love trauma) takes a lot.

When someone has been through a toxic or abusive relationship, or even just a relationship where they were repeatedly made to feel "less than," the emotional and psychological impact often results in what I call "life-constriction." It shrinks the possibilities you feel brave enough to consider. It silences your desires. It dulls your joy. And it whispers lies about who you are and what you're capable of doing.

You may stop dreaming. You may stop reaching. You may start believing that your world is smaller than it really is. Not because it *is* but because the trauma narrowed your view and tightened your sense of freedom.

And in this way, trauma constricts our possibility. When someone is repeatedly criticized, manipulated, gaslit, or emotionally harmed by a partner, over time, the message lands: *I am not enough. I can't trust myself. I'm not capable of doing the things I once thought I could.* And what's even more insidious is that it often doesn't feel like a thought. It actually feels like a fact.

Maybe you were told that you're bad at making friends, that you're too much or not enough, that no one will love you the way this person does. Maybe you were made to feel incompetent at work or mocked for your dreams. Maybe you were told, either subtly or blatantly, that you're not beautiful, desirable, smart, or lovable. And maybe, over time, you started believing it.

That belief system? It doesn't stay isolated in the past. It echoes very loudly. It shows up every time you hesitate to say yes to an opportunity. Every time you feel anxious in a social setting. Every time you have an idea but don't speak it aloud. Every time you dream something big but quickly talk yourself out of it.

This is why *corrective experiences* are so vital. They help you *disprove the illusion* that trauma hardwired into your mind and nervous system.

Let me introduce you to a former client of mine. Let's call her Brooke. Brooke was bright, funny, and deeply caring. At her core, she was a naturally social, magnetic person. But by the time we met, she had stopped going to gatherings altogether. She avoided parties, dreaded networking events, and declined invitations, even from close friends. Her world had become small and lonely. And she blamed herself for that.

Brooke's ex-partner made it a routine to rip her apart after every social event. If she laughed too loud, he mocked her. If she shared a story, he told her she embarrassed herself. If someone paid her a compliment, he twisted it into something shameful. After parties, he would corner her at home and replay everything she said, highlighting every "mistake," every misstep, real or imagined. This sometimes went on for hours.

Eventually, Brooke stopped putting herself in situations where she could be scrutinized. She decided she just wasn't a social person. She convinced herself that she was awkward, boring, and unlikable.

But the truth? That version of her was never real. It was a story carefully constructed by someone who benefited from her staying small. A story crafted in trauma.

As we worked together, I introduced Brooke to the concept of *corrective experiences*. These are experiences that directly challenge the false beliefs and trauma-based programming by gently exposing you to the very things you've been avoiding.

We began slowly. I first helped her reconnect with her nervous system. Through the process, I was teaching her grounding techniques, breathwork, and self-soothing tools to reduce anxiety and help her stay present when fear or shame tried to hijack the moment. Once she had a few tools in her back pocket, we planned for her to attend a small social gathering, one where she could bring a supportive friend.

Afterward, instead of self-criticizing or replaying every interaction, Brooke journaled about what *went well.* She practiced self-compassion. She let herself notice when someone smiled at her, laughed at her joke, or sought out her company.

And here's the beautiful thing: She didn't just survive. She lit up. Her nervous system began to recognize, "This is safe now. This is who I really am." And with every new social moment she leaned into, she reclaimed more of the vibrant woman she had once been, long before trauma convinced her otherwise.

Corrective experiences are more than just doing the things that scare you. They are about showing your nervous system, over and over again, that the threat it's expecting is no longer real. That you're no longer in that dangerous relationship. That you're safe to show up, take up space, and be fully you.

Neuroscience backs this up. When we experience trauma, our brain creates associations between certain experiences and danger. But these associations don't disappear just because the trauma is over. In fact, the more we avoid those experiences, the stronger the fear becomes.

But when we *intentionally* expose ourselves gently, safely, with support to the things we've been avoiding, we *rewire* our brains. Our internal alarms stop going off. Our sense of agency grows. And our belief in ourselves begins to rebuild. Not just intellectually but somatically. In the body. Where deep and lasting healing happens.

Your Turn: Reclaiming What's Yours

Let me ask you a few questions, gently and honestly:

- What are you avoiding right now, not because you don't want it but because you're afraid?
- What part of your life feels smaller than you know it could be?
- What desires have you buried because someone once told you that you weren't good enough?

Now, ask yourself: *What do I long to welcome back in?*

Maybe it's community. Maybe it's love. Maybe it's singing in public again, or going back to school, or allowing yourself to be seen, really seen, for the first time in a long time. Maybe it's dating, dancing, acting, applying for a job you feel unqualified for, or traveling solo. Whatever it is, it matters. Because what trauma took from you, *you have the power to take back.*

Making It Happen

Here's how to begin:

- **Name it.** Identify one thing you deeply want that fear or trauma has talked you out of getting or achieving.
- **Plan for it.** Find one small way to move toward that thing. Research it. Book it. Schedule it. Write it in your calendar.
- **Tool up.** Choose which strategies you'll use to stay present. Will you journal before and after? Will you use breathwork beforehand? Will you text a friend for support?
- **Go gently.** This is not about forcing or pushing. It's about choosing. Choose something that feels brave *but possible.* Let your healing pace be sacred.
- **Repeat it.** The power of corrective experiences builds through repetition. With each step, your nervous system gets the memo: *This is safe now. I'm free to live.*

You don't have to believe a new story all at once. Sometimes, the mind can't be convinced through words alone. But when your *body* gets the memo through lived, felt experiences, healing becomes real. New neural pathways open. And new beliefs begin to bloom.

You are not broken. You are not incapable. You are not unlovable or too much or not enough.

That was never the truth. The truth is this:

You are capable of creating the life you long for.
You always have been.
You just forgot for a little while.

So, go ahead. Reclaim what's yours. Step back into the light. Seek out the experiences that prove your fears wrong and your power right.

PART THREE

claiming your manifestation mind

Reconnecting with your intuitive voice can take time. But when you rebuild that bond, something extraordinary happens. You stop outsourcing your truth.

restoring your intuition
for manifestation

One of the deepest and most disorienting injuries that love trauma inflicts is the severing of our connection to our own intuitive voice. For many survivors, this break doesn't happen all at once. It's gradual, like a dimmer switch slowly turning down until you're standing in the dark, unsure of where you are. That quiet, wise inner voice that once whispered truth, guidance, and gut instincts becomes faint, distorted, or completely drowned out.

This disconnection is one of the most common and painful aftereffects of love trauma. And it happens for many reasons. Some of those reasons are very dramatic, and others are surprisingly subtle. In overtly abusive relationships, there's often a strategic and sustained campaign to separate the survivor from their own knowing. Gaslighting is one of the main tools used to accomplish this. Over time, the survivor begins to question their memories, emotions, and perceptions. "Maybe I *am* overreacting." "Maybe I misunderstood." "Maybe it's *me*." These thoughts don't come from a place of clarity. They are symptoms of a psychological warfare waged against their inner wisdom.

The abusive partner often views their partner's intuition as a threat, because it is. Intuition is the doorway to autonomy, discernment, and boundaries. It's the part of you that *knows* when something isn't right even if you can't yet explain why. And because abusers often rely on confusion and compliance to maintain control, they launch a full-scale attack on that inner wisdom. They chip away at it with subtle doubts and overt accusations, until the survivor is left in a fog of self-doubt.

But this intuitive disconnection doesn't only happen in abusive relationships. It's just as prevalent (though often harder to identify) in quietly toxic dynamics too. Relationships where one partner is constantly over-functioning, chronically accommodating, or living in a state of hypervigilance to avoid upsetting the other. Over time, the habit of attending to everyone else's needs while ignoring your own teaches the nervous system: *Other people's desires are more important than what you need.*

Eventually, that habit becomes a way of life. Your inner voice, the one that used to tug at your sleeve or whisper warnings, becomes muted by years of prioritizing external validation over internal guidance.

You lose the sound of your own knowing.

And yet one of the most remarkable turning points in a survivor's healing journey is the moment they begin to *hear* that voice again. The moment they not only *feel* their intuition stirring but actually *trust* it enough to follow where it leads.

This reconnection is not just symbolic. It's foundational. I watch for it as a sign that someone is truly reclaiming their inner authority.

Let me show you what that looks like.

When I began working with Holly, she was caught in the thick fog of self-doubt. Her relationship with her husband had been deeply damaging. It was filled with emotional manipulation, criticism, and cycles of fear and guilt. But more than anything, what hurt the most was that she no longer trusted herself.

"I should have known better," she said over and over. "Why didn't I see it? Why didn't I listen to myself?"

She wasn't just grieving the pain of the relationship. She was grieving the loss of her own inner compass.

As we worked together, we began to explore the idea that her intuitive voice hadn't been *wrong*, it had simply been *overridden*. That small, quiet voice inside her had *always* been there, nudging her with gut feelings, dreams, discomfort, and even anxiety. But like so many survivors, she had overridden it, because listening to it would have meant acknowledging a painful truth she wasn't ready to face.

It wasn't her intuition that failed her. It was the context of fear, hope, and conditioning that convinced her to silence it. As she began to understand this, something powerful started to shift.

She moved from self-blame to self-compassion. From doubt to curiosity. And slowly, she began experimenting with listening to that quiet voice again. At first, she practiced with small things such as choosing what she wanted for dinner, noticing when her body tensed around certain people, following her gut about which route to take home. She didn't need proof or logic, just the willingness to tune in.

Over time, that voice grew stronger. She could recognize it not only in her thoughts but also in her body and the way her stomach tightened or her chest lifted with ease. She learned that intuition doesn't always speak in words. Sometimes, it's a sensation. A pull. A pause. A knowing without knowing how. Today, Holly trusts her intuition like an old friend. She doesn't need to justify it. She just listens. And that listening has become one of the greatest acts of self-love.

> ### *Think of your intuition like a lighthouse on a rocky shore. Even when the storm is raging and the waves are crashing, that light is still turning.*

But if you've been caught in a storm long enough, you might forget it's there. You might think you imagined it. Or worse. You might have been told there *was never* a lighthouse at all.

That's what emotional abuse and chronic invalidation do: they make you doubt the light. But the lighthouse never left.

The work of healing is not about *building* a new intuitive voice, it's about *clearing the fog* so you can see and feel the one that has always been guiding you.

If you're in the process of healing from love trauma, it's time to gently begin restoring your relationship with your intuitive self. Listening to the whispers and nudges of your intuitive voice is an extraordinary manifestation tool. It helps you to clue in to what feels like what you truly want and what feels "off." It helps you to listen in to the little signals that you're on the right track and going in the directions of your desires. It helps you to truly know when you want something versus being programmed to believe you want it. And for all these reasons, reclaiming your intuitive voice is a powerful manifestation technique that should not be overlooked.

HERE ARE A FEW WAYS TO BEGIN:

1. Describe Your Relationship with Your Intuition

If your intuition were a person, how would you describe your relationship with them?

- Are you giving them the silent treatment?
- Do you dismiss them when they speak?
- Do you constantly second-guess them?
- Or are you warm, open, curious, and willing to hear what they have to say?

2. Create a Visual or Symbol

Imagine your intuition as a symbol, like a glowing orb in your chest, a wise elder, a quiet river, a tuning fork. What would it look like? How does it feel?

Visualize this symbol in moments of stillness, and return to it often, like a meditation. Even one minute a day can begin to rewire the way you relate to your own knowing.

3. Notice, Don't Judge

Start by simply noticing when your intuition shows up. Maybe it's a quick gut feeling, a subtle discomfort, a sense of déjà vu, or a sudden clarity.

Don't try to analyze or act on it right away. Just notice it, name it, and say: *I hear you.*

That tiny moment of recognition is the beginning of repair.

Reconnecting with your intuitive voice isn't always immediate. It can take time, tenderness, and a willingness to sit with discomfort.

But when you rebuild that bond, something extraordinary happens.

You stop outsourcing your truth.

You begin to walk through the world with a grounded sense of self—one that can sense danger, recognize alignment, and choose what feels nourishing.

That voice inside you is not broken. It is not lost. It is simply waiting for you to come back home.

And when you do?

You don't just heal from love trauma—you step into the most powerful love of all: the one between *you* and *yourself.*

heartbundance

Your capacity is not something you have to fabricate.
It's something you remember.
And in that remembering, you find yourself
on your way toward manifesting.

rediscovering your capacity

There comes a quiet but pivotal moment in the healing journey that has a major impact on building a manifestation mind. This is a moment that often arrives not with fireworks or fanfare but with a whisper:

Maybe I can.

Maybe I *can* do this. Maybe I *can* rebuild. Maybe I *can* manifest a life that feels expansive and loving and free.

When you've survived a relationship steeped in emotional abuse, manipulation, or subtle toxicity, that whisper may come wrapped in doubt, barely audible under the noise of internalized messages that told you for so long: *You're not enough. You're incapable. It won't happen for you.*

Those messages that came from gaslighting, neglect, and control may have buried your capacity under layers of distortion. They didn't erase your power, but they covered it up.

And so, when we talk about manifesting after trauma, we have to begin with something deeper than wishful thinking or surface affirmations. We start something more foundational and sacred: a *reassessment of capacity.*

In the aftermath of love trauma, it's not uncommon to feel like you've lost your edge. Like something vital inside you has gone dim. You might hesitate before applying for a new job, questioning whether you're smart or competent enough. You might avoid trying to make new friends, fearing your zest for social events has withered. You might shy away from setting bold goals, thinking: *That's for someone stronger or more confident than me.*

These feelings are understandable. They are echoes of what you were conditioned to believe when your needs were minimized, when your voice was silenced, or when your gifts were overlooked or used against you. Abusive and toxic relationships have a way of eroding the self without you even realizing it. It doesn't just hurt. It *hollows.* And in that hollowing, it carves a false narrative: *You are less than. You are incapable.*

But the real truth is this:

Your capacity was never lost.
It was only covered.

There's a bridge between reclaiming your sense of capacity and manifestation. But let's start at the beginning for now. Many manifestation teachings ask us to "just believe," meaning to hold a high vibration, to think positively, and to align with the version of us who already has it all.

But if you've been through trauma, this can feel hollow. Or worse, shame-inducing.

Because how do you align with a version of yourself you no longer recognize? How do you believe in success or abundance when your nervous system still flinches in the presence of hope?

The answer is: *You don't leap. You build.* You build the bridge between where you are and where you want to be, one reclaimed belief at a time. And that bridge is built every time you claim another piece of your own capacity back again.

To reassess your capacity doesn't mean forcing yourself to be more than you are. It means asking, with curiosity and compassion:

- *What am I actually capable of right now?*
- *What limiting beliefs am I carrying from my past experiences?*
- *Is the story I'm telling myself about my abilities still true?*

Maybe you discover that you're more emotionally resilient than you realized. Maybe you notice that, while social anxiety still lingers, you're beginning to enjoy small talk again. Maybe you attempt something new, like hosting a party for friends, taking a class, or starting a business. And even if it doesn't go perfectly, it goes. And in that process, you will grow too.

This is how you organically *strengthen the muscle of self-belief.* Not by denying where you are but by gently stretching into more possibilities.

Leah, a client of mine, spent ten years in a relationship where her dreams were belittled and her decisions were constantly second-guessed. By the time she left, she wasn't sure if she could make a dentist appointment without having a panic attack.

In the early days of healing, manifestation felt out of reach. When she read books that told her to just "think big," she felt like she was failing.

So, instead of leaping, she leaned in. She began small: journaling daily, celebrating when she made phone calls, slowly reconnecting with her creativity by painting abstract images of her emotions.

One day, she realized: "I don't feel like I'm faking it anymore. I feel like I'm *becoming* it." She hadn't forced confidence. Instead, she *earned* her way back to it by removing the emotional debris in its way.

Think of this time, when you're rediscovering your capacity, as a sacred reintroduction. Instead of demanding greatness from yourself, get curious about your rediscovered strengths and abilities.

Approach your capacity like an archaeologist brushing dust off ancient treasure. Let it be a process of discovery, not proof. Try something new. Let it be messy. Let it surprise you.

Refrain from expecting yourself to be Superwoman overnight. You don't need to *prove* your power. You just need to *uncover* it.

If your perception of your own capacity still feels small, that's okay. That's not failure. That's a sign you're telling the truth. Meet yourself there. Be honest about where you're starting from and excited about where you're going. You don't have to reclaim everything at once. But you *do* have to keep going.

Keep healing.
Keep transmuting.
Keep reassessing.
And eventually, the tide will turn.

Let me leave you with this truth tucked into your heart like a note you find later on a hard day:

Your capacity is not something you have to fabricate.
It is something you remember.

And in that remembering, you'll find yourself on your way toward manifesting. Because believing that you can is one of the foundational tenets of how to move your desires from a thought into physical reality.

JOURNAL PROMPTS:

1. What do I believe I'm capable of right now, and where might that belief be limited by my past?
2. What areas of my life feel like they need a reassessment?
3. Where have I surprised myself recently with growth or resilience?
4. If I were meeting myself for the first time today, what strengths would I notice?

Let this be your gentle return to your own capacity, and the beginning of your manifestation mind. One grounded, sacred step at a time.

*Manifestation doesn't begin with affirmations
or vision boards. It begins with the deep,
cellular knowing that you are worthy of receiving.*

worthiness:
the forgotten key to manifestation

There is a truth about healing from love trauma that many people don't realize until they're already knee-deep in the work: it's not just about what happened to you, it's about what you came to believe about yourself because of it.

When you've survived the deep cuts of love trauma (especially the kind that unfold slowly, quietly, and over time), not only your sense of your capacity may become dulled. You stop believing that you're powerful, that you're capable, that you're the kind of person who can steer your life toward something beautiful and bold.

There's also something even deeper, more tender, and often even more injured than your belief in your capacity. It's your belief in your *worthiness*. And this is one of the most underestimated and foundational aspects of shifting from the "love wound mind" into the "manifestation mind."

Abusive relationships and toxic love relationships often erode your self-esteem. In more explosive relationships, the assault is obvious: You're told outright that you're too much, too little, unlovable, crazy, or broken. The pain is sharp, blatant, and brutal.

But in the quietly toxic relationships, the damage is more like a slow leak. It's harder to notice and often, easier to justify. You notice a small, jarring comment here. A subtle withdrawal there. A pattern of being dismissed, minimized, or overlooked. It doesn't scream, it whispers. But the effect over time is devastating. It wears away at your self-regard like waves eroding the foundation of a cliff. And then one day that cliff collapses, and you don't know who you are anymore.

You no longer feel like someone deserving of goodness. And this is where manifestation breaks down. It's not because the Universe isn't listening, and not because you're doing it "wrong." It feels like you're abandoned by the Universe because there's a quiet part of you that no longer believes you're worthy of receiving what you're asking for.

Manifestation doesn't begin with forcing yourself to see an outcome that doesn't feel attainable or to artificially convince yourself that something will happen. You cannot trick your brain and soul to believe something that feels out of reach. Instead, it begins with the deep, cellular knowing that you are worthy of receiving. Without this deeply rooted knowing, your desires might feel like faraway fantasies rather than actual possibilities. Your mind might say, *I want this,* while your energy whispers, *But I don't deserve it.*

That inner conflict (the energetic difference between your desire and your perceived worthiness) is often the invisible wall that keeps what you long for just out of reach. So, let's get to the core.

You don't have to earn your worthiness.

You were born with it.

A newborn baby isn't worthy because she's achieved anything. She's not valuable because she hit a milestone, or said the right thing, or made someone proud. She's worthy simply because she *is*. She breathes, she exists, and that is enough.

So, what about you?

What made you forget that you are already enough?

The truth is, life (and especially traumatic love) can teach you lies. It can convince you that you are only lovable when you perform, when you please, when you give up your needs, when you dim your light, when you shrink. But these are survival adaptations, not reflections of your worth.

And because you're reading this now, know this:

Your worth never left you.

It may have been buried. But it is still there, intact, whole, waiting for you to remember.

I once worked with a client named Celeste. She's a brilliant, capable woman who had built a wildly successful business from the ground up. On paper, she had everything: wealth, influence, talent, drive. But after years of emotional abuse from a partner who constantly undermined and manipulated her, Celeste's sense of self had withered. The outside world saw a powerhouse. But inside? She felt like a fraud. Even after she left the relationship, the residue of that abuse followed her like a shadow. Her mind told her she could create anything, but her heart couldn't believe she deserved it. She found herself sabotaging opportunities, staying in toxic dynamics, and second-guessing every decision.

The real shift came when we stopped focusing on external goalposts and started tending to the soft, trembling place inside her that questioned her worthiness to receive. Together, we worked on a daily ritual. It was a meditation on *inherent worth*. She began by visualizing herself as a newborn. No accolades, no accomplishments. Just her, in her purest form. She imagined herself being held, seen, cherished, and safe. No needing to earn it. Just being, and being enough.

Over time, that daily meditation softened the walls around her heart. It began to rewire her beliefs. And something remarkable happened: She started seeing possibilities again. Real, tangible shifts began unfolding in business opportunities, friendships, love that felt nurturing rather than draining. Her manifestation energy came online, and not because she forced it but because she finally believed she was allowed to have what she wanted.

Think of yourself as a vessel. If you don't believe you're worthy, it's like trying to fill a vessel full of cracks. No matter how much goodness the Universe pours into you, it leaks out through the fractures in your self-regard.

But when you patch those cracks through remembrance, gentleness, and truth, you become a sturdy container. And suddenly all that abundance, love, opportunity, and joy? It has somewhere to stay. It can finally land.

Practical Ways to Rebuild Worthiness

Reclaiming your worth doesn't happen in one big moment. It happens in layers—in tiny, repeated acts of remembrance. Here are a few ways to start:

1. Daily Truth Practice

Each morning, place your hand over your heart and whisper:

"I am worthy because I exist. My worth is not up for debate."

Let that be your anchor as you move through your day.

2. Visual Meditation

Picture yourself as a child: innocent, vibrant, untouched by conditioning. Imagine wrapping her in light. Speak to her as you would to a beloved being: "You are safe. You are good. You matter." This can help reprogram the subconscious mind.

3. Catch the Saboteur Voice

When you notice self-critical thoughts creeping in, pause. Ask, "Whose voice is this?" Often, you'll realize it's not even yours. It's an echo of someone who never saw you clearly. Gently choose not to believe it anymore.

4. Practice Receiving

Say *yes* when someone offers help. Let yourself be complimented without deflecting. Treat yourself to something without justifying it. These are not indulgences, they are recalibrations of your deservedness.

5. Use the Mirror

Each night, look into your own eyes in the mirror and say: "You are already enough. I see you. I love you. I believe in you." This may feel strange at first, but over time, it becomes medicine.

Above all, remember this: **You are not the one human for whom worthiness doesn't apply. You are not the one who must earn what others are simply allowed to receive.**

Your worth is your birthright. Your self-regard is the soil from which your dreams will grow. The more you nourish it, the more you will become a magnet for the life you're longing to live.

Because manifestation isn't just about believing in the dream. It's about believing you belong to it.

heartbundance

Excavating the parts of you that were buried
because of love trauma is a power move. It's not about
remembering who you were, but more about reclaiming
the parts of you that were buried.

excavating your hidden parts

In the aftermath of abusive or quietly toxic love, one of the most tender and soul-restoring journeys is rediscovering the parts of yourself you buried just to survive.

For many survivors, especially those who endured prolonged emotional abuse, the cost of "belonging" in the relationship came at the expense of authenticity. To preserve the bond, you had to become a contortionist of the soul. Bending. Folding. Shrinking. Shapeshifting.

And often, you didn't even realize you were doing it.

Maybe you were the type of person who once sparkled when you walked into a room. You had stories to tell, laughter to share, ideas that lit up your mind like constellations. But somewhere along the way, your light started dimming. And not because it faded but because you were slowly convinced that shining too brightly would burn someone else. So, you learned to stay small. To whisper instead of sing. To retreat instead of radiate. Let's call this dynamic what it is: survival patterning. And it often forms without conscious awareness.

Survivors of love trauma, especially those who've been in relationships marked by control, manipulation, or coercion, often find themselves slowly molding to meet the unspoken "rules" of the relationship. These rules are invisible lines drawn in the sand:

Don't be too successful, don't be too outspoken, don't be too happy, don't be too seen.

Why? Because the more *you* you were, the more conflict it created.

If your joy made them feel inadequate, you learned to laugh a little less. If your success made them feel threatened, you downplayed your dreams. If your natural charisma made them insecure, you became the quieter one in the room. Not because you were weak but because you were wise enough to survive.

Let's be clear: this kind of shapeshifting isn't cowardly. It was your nervous system doing everything it could to keep you safe. And in the moment, it *did* reduce tension. It *did* maintain the illusion of harmony. But over time, it did something else too. It buried parts of you.

In these kinds of relationships, your personality, passions, and potential are filtered through one question: *Is this safe to show?* So, you become what I call a "relational chameleon." You had to change colors to blend into someone else's emotional climate. It was safer to become a finely tuned mirror, reflecting only what's palatable, what won't provoke, what won't invite punishment or withdrawal. It's not that you lost yourself, it's that parts of who you are got sealed away in a protective vault.

When healing begins, and your nervous system starts to uncoil from its trauma patterning, you may begin to sense something stirring like a buried seed pushing upward toward light. This is the moment when the excavation begins.

Excavation is a gentle yet powerful process. It's not just about remembering who you were but about reclaiming the parts of you that were buried. And yes, it can be emotional. Sometimes it feels like meeting a long-lost part of yourself that you didn't even realize was missing.

And here's the truth that's both sacred and heartbreaking:

The things you had to hide are often the brightest parts of your soul.

Let me share the story of one of my clients. Let's call her Danielle. Danielle was brilliant. She's sharp, intuitive, and wildly capable when it comes to business. But she ended up in a relationship with a man who was deeply threatened by her competence. To maintain control, he insisted she work *for him* not *with him*. And every day, he micromanaged her, belittled her, questioned her skills, until she started doubting herself.

Even though she was running the operations of his business, he made sure she felt like a failure. So, what did she do? Like many survivors, Danielle hid her brilliance, even from herself. She internalized his voice until it became her own. She began to believe she wasn't capable of leading anything on her own. But once Danielle left that relationship and began the healing process, something incredible happened. As her nervous system softened and she began to feel safe again, she could finally look back and see clearly: She was never incompetent. She was extraordinary.

And that realization was electric. She started her own business. Within a year, it flourished. And each success was not just a professional victory, it was a sacred act of reclamation.

Danielle wasn't becoming someone new. She was finally allowed to reclaim her hidden, brilliant parts that were so threatening to that partner from her past.

When you're in a love wound mind, you subconsciously make choices from fear, from self-protection, from the need to keep the peace. But when you begin stepping into a manifestation mind, the whole landscape changes. You're no longer editing yourself to be acceptable. You are actively *amplifying* who you are.

To do this, you must excavate the parts of yourself that were once deemed "too much." Too loud. Too successful. Too opinionated. Too radiant.

ASK YOURSELF:

- What traits did I feel I had to hide in that relationship?
- What aspects of myself did I water down, silence, or shrink?
- Where did I dim my light because it threatened someone else's shadow?

Then lovingly, tenderly, *bring those parts back into the light.*

Imagine your true self like an ornate tapestry that had been folded up and stored in the attic of your soul. Dusty, hidden, forgotten. The abusive relationship said, "Don't hang this. Don't show this. It makes me uncomfortable."

But now, you're unrolling it. Letting the light hit it again. Seeing the colors, the detail, the vibrancy.

Or imagine yourself as a violin: once silenced by someone who feared your song. Now, your fingers find the strings again, and the melody that emerges isn't just music. It's a memory. It's *magic.*

This is what it means to reclaim your hidden parts after love trauma. It's not just about healing wounds. It's about retrieving your gifts.

It probably doesn't surprise you to learn that the very traits you had to hide are often the ones most essential to your next chapter. Your confidence. Your charisma. Your intuition. Your creativity. Your ambition. These are not problems to be managed—they are *portals* to your purpose.

As you step into your manifestation mind, it's not about becoming someone new. Instead, it's about becoming more of who you already are, unapologetically.

Because here's the beautiful truth:

What you hid to survive, you will now use to thrive.

JOURNAL PROMPTS FOR EXCAVATING THE HIDDEN SELF:

1. What parts of myself did I feel were "too much" in past relationships?
2. What traits, talents, or desires did I have to suppress to maintain the relationship?
3. In what ways did I become smaller, quieter, or less visible to feel safe?
4. What would it feel like to bring those traits into the light now?
5. If I were no longer afraid of threatening someone with my brilliance, what would I do?
6. What's one part of myself I'm ready to reclaim starting today?

This chapter is not just about reflecting; instead, it's about *resurrecting*. Because your power, your joy, your voice . . . none of it was lost. It was simply waiting for you to come back for it.

Stepping into your manifestation mind is not only about reclaiming the parts of you that were buried.
It's also about releasing the parts of you that were created to help protect you, which now constrict you.

releasing what was never yours to keep

There is a sacred, often overlooked counterpart to the process of rediscovering your true self after surviving emotional abuse or love-based trauma. It's not only about *reclaiming* the parts of you that were buried, it is also equally about *releasing* the parts of you that were never truly yours to begin with.

These are the coping traits you *had* to develop to survive. The masks. The shrinking. The silencing. The smallness. The safety mechanisms that kept you afloat in a relationship where love had strings attached, where who you *truly were* became a liability.

Think of yourself as a tree. In an abusive or quietly toxic relationship, you may have been forced to grow sideways, toward the only bit of light that was allowed. You bent yourself. Maybe your roots twisted to accommodate rocky soil, your branches contorted toward conditional love. That growth was real, yes, but it wasn't *natural*. It wasn't *you*.

Healing asks that you not only turn back toward your natural light but that you also *prune away* the distorted growth. You must shed what was built under duress. The traits you learned to protect yourself (like self-silencing, people-pleasing, risk aversion, hypervigilance, or constant second-guessing) may have served you once. But now, they stand as walls between you and your fullest expression. They clash with your manifestation mind, that part of you that knows how to create, expand, and receive.

Let's be clear: Many of these traits didn't arise from weakness. They came from wisdom, from your body and soul doing whatever it took to preserve peace, to avoid conflict, to stay safe. But peace that costs you *yourself* is not peace. It's prison.

Think of a bird that's convinced herself her cage is a sanctuary. She's learned to fly in small loops. She no longer dreams of sky. Her feathers grow dull, not from lack of beauty but from lack of use. The traits you've developed to survive (such as denying your instincts, muting your needs, or minimizing your dreams) are like that cage. They may have kept you "safe," but they have also kept you from flying.

To reclaim your inner Creator, your Manifestor, your *fully expressed self*, you must not only recover what was buried, you must *burn away* what does not belong.

Let me bring this home with a story. One of my clients, Jason, was a vibrant, opinionated, and passionate man. He had a strong sense of self and didn't hesitate to speak his mind. But over time, in a relationship that seemed loving on the outside but was subtly corrosive on the inside, Jason learned that his assertiveness provoked backlash. His partner would respond with emotional withdrawal, criticism, and threats of abandonment. The message was clear: "If you want peace, you need to tone it down."

And so, he did.

He began to edit himself. He measured his words. He kept quiet even when disrespected. He smiled when he wanted to scream. Over the years, assertiveness was replaced with a new trait that replaced it: submission.

In our work together, I helped him recognize that he gained submission through his trauma, and it was time to release it with his mindful awareness and pattern interruption. Bit by bit, Jason began to speak up again. At first in therapy, then with friends, and finally, with his wife. And it was powerful.

But the healing didn't stop there.

Shedding submission wouldn't have worked, and *couldn't* have lasted, if we hadn't also helped Jason *shed* the belief that keeping the peace was his responsibility. We had to challenge the deeper lie that "love means quieting yourself for someone else's comfort." That belief wasn't his truth. It was planted in him by fear and control. And it had to be uprooted.

Because what good is finding your voice if you still believe it's dangerous to speak?

Imagine trying to drive with one foot on the gas and the other on the brake. That's what happens when you shed protective traits but still hold on to the survival beliefs that say, "Don't go too far. Don't be too much. Don't upset the balance." You end up stalled, stuck between expansion and contraction.

This is why both sides of the healing equation are essential:

- Shed the protective traits that aren't really "you."
- Release the beliefs that led to those protective traits developing in the first place.

> *Manifestation is about embodying*
> *the energy of creation itself.*
> *And creation requires expansion.*

It asks that you stop contorting yourself to fit into someone else's narrow idea of who you should be. It invites you to stretch. To rise. To take up space. To be loud if you're loud, quiet if you're quiet, bold if you're bold. You can't create a vibrant, authentic life from a place of suppression where you continue to hold on to constrictive, protective traits that are keeping you small. You must reclaim your fire, but you must also *stop pouring water on it.*

A New Way Forward

Here's what this process might look like:

- **You shed second-guessing** and reclaim your inner authority.
- **You release self-silencing** and reclaim your voice.
- **You let go of being small** and reclaim your space in the world.
- **You burn the belief that "conflict is dangerous"** and reclaim the truth that "boundaries are sacred."
- **You stop contorting for peace** and reclaim the wild, divine chaos of your authentic self.

And every time you do this, even in the smallest way, you move closer to the manifestation mind.

Picture yourself stepping out of a costume that no longer fits. It's a costume that once protected you but now stifles your breath. As you shed it, your skin breathes. Your spirit stretches. Your heart takes up more room in your chest. You're not becoming someone new. You're becoming *you*, finally.

The one who was there all along.

And that version of you? She. He. They. This version of you creates worlds.

JOURNAL PROMPTS FOR SHEDDING THE FALSE SELF:

1. What traits or behaviors did you adopt that you now recognize as "protective traits"?
2. If you had never experienced that relationship, how would you naturally show up in the world?
3. What would it feel like to live without those protective traits that came from your love trauma? Describe a day in your life as your fully expressed self.
4. Write a goodbye letter to one protective trait you're ready to release. Thank it. Then let it go.

Trying to manifest without personal boundaries
is like trying to build on land
you don't yet believe belongs to you.

reclaiming your boundaries for the manifestation mind

One of the most powerful and often overlooked steps in cultivating the manifestation mind after surviving love abuse is reclaiming your right to boundaries in how you establish them, honor them, and consistently uphold them. For many survivors of love trauma, boundaries feel like a dangerous luxury, or worse, an offense punishable by silence, withdrawal, or outright rage.

Let's be honest: Boundaries have not always felt safe. In fact, for most survivors, boundaries were one of the things that got them punished. Whether through manipulation, guilt-tripping, stonewalling, or explosive reactions, you may have learned that taking space (whether it was emotional, physical, or mental) was not just frowned upon, it was framed as a betrayal. You might have been told, "You're selfish," "You're too much," "Why do you need that?" or, perhaps more cruelly, your needs were simply met with silence or abandonment.

So, it's no wonder that setting boundaries can feel terrifying. Even if no one is actively crossing you anymore, your nervous system might still be wired to expect retaliation. You might even anticipate guilt like a thunderstorm on the horizon whenever you even *think* about asserting yourself.

But boundaries are not walls. They are not weapons. And they are not selfish.

> **Boundaries are bridges.**
> **They're sacred structures that lead you**
> **from the trauma-patterned mind**
> **to the empowered, manifesting self.**

Imagine trying to build a house, but every time you set down a brick, someone else moves it or tells you that you shouldn't build at all. Now imagine that you internalized their voice and began questioning whether you deserved the house to begin with. That's what it's like to try to manifest your vision without boundaries. You're trying to build on land you don't yet believe belongs to you.

Boundaries are the *foundation* upon which your vision takes root. They declare: *This is where I begin and you end. This is what I need and will no longer apologize for. This is what I will protect because it is sacred to me.*

If you don't have the space to breathe, to dream, and to choose your own direction, you can't create with your vision intact. It might be someone else's vision, someone else's needs, someone else's path. And that is the quiet tragedy of boundarylessness: we become caretakers of other people's dreams and abandon our own.

One of the clearest symptoms of a boundary-starved life is chronic exhaustion. You feel drained and buried. You feel like your dreams and aspirations are constantly getting postponed in favor of someone else's.

You may find yourself people-pleasing, over-functioning, always "on," always accommodating and never fully having the time or energetic spaciousness to plant the seeds of your desires, let alone water them into fruition.

This is not laziness. This is not lack of drive. This is the *invisible labor* of managing everyone else's expectations while silencing your own truth. It's the spiritual equivalent of trying to write your story with someone else's pen, on someone else's timeline.

You cannot manifest what you do not believe you're allowed to have. And you cannot create what you do not have room to nurture. Ask yourself: Do I feel entitled to my own space? This might be the most important question in this entire chapter:

Do you feel deeply, inherently, unquestionably—that you have a right to your own boundaries?

If your answer isn't a whole-hearted, resounding *yes*, then it's time to get curious.

- Where did you learn otherwise?
- Who taught you that your needs were negotiable?
- What happened when you tried to protect your energy, your space, your time?
- Were your boundaries dismissed, mocked, punished?
- Did you receive mixed signals—"Yes, of course you can say no," followed by coldness, withdrawal, or passive-aggression?

Manifestation requires *space and time*. It requires energy, clarity, vision, and action. It requires you to show up for your desires with consistency and courage.

You cannot do that if your energy is being siphoned off by obligations that don't serve you. You cannot do that if your mental bandwidth is taken up by guilt, people-pleasing, or navigating the emotional landmines of others. You cannot do that if you are too afraid to claim time to sit in your own stillness, to hear your own voice, to follow your own inspiration.

Boundaries are not a sidenote. They are the *prerequisite* for the manifestation mind.

They are how you carve out sacred space in a chaotic world and say: *Here, in this space, I choose. I create. I become.*

> **When you say no to something that drains you, you're saying yes to something that fulfills you.**

When you step back from a relationship that violates your peace, you're stepping toward one that honors your truth. When you guard your energy like it is a flame worth protecting, it grows into a wildfire of transformation.

Healthy people will not be threatened by your boundaries. Only those who benefited from your boundarylessness will push back. Let that be your compass.

Affirming Your Right to Manifest Through Boundaries

Say this aloud, if you can. Say it to your reflection. Say it as a prayer.

My space is sacred.
My needs are valid.
My boundaries are not barriers, they're bridges to my future.
I deserve to choose how I use my time, my energy, my life.

I am allowed to protect what I am building.

I am allowed to say no.

I am allowed to say yes to me.

JOURNAL PROMPTS TO EXPLORE YOUR BOUNDARIES:

1. Do I believe I have the right to my own boundaries? If not, where did I learn that belief?
2. What were boundaries like in my family growing up?
3. Can I recall moments in past relationships when my boundaries were punished or ignored? How did that shape me?
4. What are some current areas in my life where I feel overextended, resentful, or drained? What boundary might need to be put in place there?
5. What do I fear will happen if I start asserting stronger boundaries? Are those fears based on past experiences or current truths?
6. What dreams or manifestations have I put on hold because I don't feel I have the time or energy for them? What boundary could help reclaim that space?

Your beliefs and your desires will shift
as you move from the love wound mind into
the manifestation mind. What once felt like enough will
now feel too small. It's time to rediscover what you want.

rediscovering what you truly desire

There comes a moment in every healing journey that is quiet, unassuming, but profound. This is when the fog around you begins to lift. You no longer feel like you're swimming through the emotional aftermath of toxic relationships, of emotionally abusive entanglements, or of partnerships that asked you to shrink. The panic has quieted. The hypervigilance softened. Your breath has begun to return to your own rhythm, not one dictated by someone else's moods or manipulations.

It is in this sacred space that a new question begins to stir:

What do I truly want?

Not what I thought I wanted when I was drowning. Not what I told myself I needed to keep the peace. Me and my own soul, unshackled.

When you're in survival mode during love trauma, your wants are filtered through a narrow lens. You may have convinced yourself that keeping the relationship intact was the deepest desire of your heart. You may have wanted a smaller job, a quieter voice, even a dimmer light, because those were the versions of you that caused the least friction. Your real voice, your bold dreams, your full aliveness? Those felt dangerous in the old dynamic. And so, your wants adjusted to what felt permissible, not what was possible.

The tricky part is that trauma doesn't just bruise your heart, it rewires your expectations. It whispers lies about what you deserve, what you're capable of, and what's available to you. It disguises limits as "realism" and dresses fear up as "maturity."

You begin to believe you're asking for too much when you're really asking for the bare minimum. You may begin to believe you're not smart enough to go after your dream job, not magnetic enough to attract real love, not strong enough to be on your own terms. You begin to dream small because small dreams feel safer.

But let's call this what it really is: emotional manipulation, often internalized and echoed back as truth. But again, this was programming. Not prophecy.

Coming out of love trauma is like walking out of a carnival house of mirrors. Inside, every reflection was warped. Your self-image stretched, shrunk, distorted until you no longer recognized the original. The dreams you dreamed in that place were based on a version of you that didn't really exist.

Now, in healing, the real mirror starts to emerge. You begin to see yourself not through their projections but through your own remembering.

And here's the question that emerges again, shimmering:

What do I want now that I am no longer looking through the lens of fear?

This part of the journey isn't about knowing your five-year plan or declaring your ultimate life purpose in perfect clarity. You don't need to write the script of the rest of your life in one sitting. Healing desire is more like listening for a melody that starts faint and gets clearer the more you attune to it.

Think of it like a garden just after winter. Some dreams are still asleep under the soil. Some are poking through with tentative shoots. And some are wildflowers you didn't even know you planted. Be patient with what's growing.

Let this be a *living question*:
What do I want when it's just me and me?
Not me and my partner.
Not me and my fears.
Not me and my trauma.
Just . . . me.

As your beliefs begin to shift as you move from the love wound mind and into the manifestation mind, you'll start to notice your desires change. What once felt like "enough" will now feel too small. What once terrified you may now feel electrifying. You'll crave expansion in places where you once settled for quiet.

You might start dreaming of starting a business, or leaving a job you outgrew, or living somewhere that feels like home to your nervous system. You might finally allow yourself to want love again—but real love, not one that costs you your peace.

You may realize that you no longer want to dim your light to keep others comfortable.

You want to shine, not to be seen, but because that's who you are.

You want to create, not to prove, because creation is your natural state.

You want to receive abundance, not just survive.

What you desire now might surprise you. It might even scare you a little. That's okay.

Desire, when rooted in truth
rather than trauma, stretches you.

It asks you to believe in your wholeness. It dares you to live as though you are already enough, which, of course, you are.

This part of expanding is sacred. It's exactly where you fine-tune what you're aiming from as you transition from the love wound mind into the manifestation mind. The version of you that no longer needs to prove their worth because you know it. The version of you that no longer needs to play small because you understand the Universe responds to your authenticity, not your perfection.

So, I invite you, gently and with reverence, to lean into this question. Revisit it often. Let it evolve as you evolve:

What do I want now that I'm no longer living under someone else's illusion of me?

The more you shed those old identities (the people-pleaser, the peacekeeper, the overachiever, the self-doubter), the clearer your own voice will sound.

JOURNAL PROMPTS TO DISCOVER YOUR TRUE DESIRES:

1. When I was surviving, what did I think I wanted? What do I realize now about those desires?

2. What parts of my old dreams were rooted in fear, safety, or approval-seeking?

3. When it's just me and me, with no one watching, what desires start to whisper to me?

4. If I fully trusted I was capable and worthy, what would I allow myself to want?

5. What feels "too big" to want right now, and why? Can I sit with the part of me that wants it anyway?

A micro step is a whisper of action in the direction of your desires. It's small enough not to rattle your nervous system yet meaningful enough to build momentum. Micro steps are the quiet architects of transformation.

the magic of micro steps
for manifestation

We live in a world obsessed with sudden breakthroughs.

Open any social media app and you'll see it. People seemingly leap overnight into millionaire status, falling into the perfect relationship after one yoga retreat, or launching six-figure businesses in a weekend. The narratives are dazzling and seductive, and they feed us a single story: that quantum leaps are not only possible but expected. But here's a truth I want you to hold close to your heart:

Real change can look like an ocean tide changing over. Slowly and steadily without you even realizing it's happening.

Yes, quantum leaps can happen. And when they do, they're beautiful. But they are the exception, not the rule. And for many of us, quantum leaps after trauma, emotional abuse, or the erosion of self-belief can be more destabilizing than liberating.

Manifestation doesn't have to be about strapping rockets to your dreams and blasting off. It's not about hurling yourself into the unknown and hoping to land on your feet. That kind of explosive change often overwhelms the nervous system, triggering fear, resistance, or even shutdown.

You're not lazy if you can't leap right now. You're not broken if you can't sprint toward your goal. You're wise to take the slow and steady approach to manifestation.

And remember, your nervous system is trying to keep you safe. Trauma taught it to be cautious. To assess before stepping. And healing means respecting that.

This is why we honor the ***micro step***. A micro step is a whisper of action in the direction of your desire. It's small enough not to rattle your nervous system yet meaningful enough to build momentum. Micro steps are the quiet architects of transformation. They are the invisible threads stitching you into the life you're creating.

Here Are Some Examples of Micro Steps:

- Writing the name of your future LLC in your Notes app.
- Spending two minutes breathing deeply and imagining how your body will feel when you're free and thriving.
- Creating one social media post to talk about your vision.
- Sending a single email to reconnect with an old friend or potential collaborator.
- Journaling about how your future self speaks, walks, and holds boundaries.

These aren't trivial actions. They're aligned, sacred ones.

Think of your dream life as a snowball rolling gently down a hill. Each micro step is a snowflake sticking to it. At first, it looks small, even unimpressive. But as it keeps rolling, with consistency and patience, it grows exponentially. It picks up speed. It becomes unstoppable.

Too many people abort the mission in the early snowball stage. They look at their tiny snowball and think, *This isn't big enough. I'm not moving fast enough. I should be further along by now.* But they don't realize that the avalanche comes from accumulation, not sudden force.

What we want is a gentle revolution. Not the kind that burns everything down in a day, but the kind that roots deeply and grows steadily, like a forest quietly taking back the land.

Here's the piece that most manifestation teachings miss:

Your nervous system must feel safe enough to receive the very thing you desire.

Let's say someone wants to start a business. If they launch the business, start taking clients, do five Instagram lives, open a payment portal, and try to monetize it all within seven days, their nervous system might go into panic.

They may find themselves suddenly tired, foggy, irritable, or unmotivated. That's not self-sabotage. It's a freeze response. They've entered uncharted waters too quickly, and the survival part of their brain is slamming the brakes.

Now imagine instead that this same person took seven months. She starts with naming her business. A few weeks later, she creates an Instagram account. The next month, she quietly shares a story about why this business matters to her. She takes time to nourish herself between each expansion. She's resting, grounding, and taking time for healing while she is expanding.

Her nervous system moves with her. There's no internal revolt, no panic button pressed. Her body feels safe enough to receive the growth. The expansion becomes sustainable. This is how we avoid snapping back to old patterns. It's not about the size of the step, it's about the consistency and alignment of the steps.

When you take a micro step, you are telling the Universe:

"I believe in this dream enough to nurture it gently."

"I believe in myself enough to build this slowly."

"I am willing to become the person who can hold this."

This isn't laziness. It's devotion. You are building a life, not a viral moment. You are cultivating roots, not just fireworks. And the deeper the roots, the higher you can grow without falling.

There will be days where you feel behind. Days when someone else's big leap will make your micro step feel insignificant. But I promise you: Every time you show up with care and consistency, you're creating compound momentum. The life you're dreaming of is already being woven under the surface. And when it blooms, it will be solid. It will last. Because it was built with love and regulated energy.

This is a spiritual truth: *Nothing truly aligned can be rushed.*

And manifestation that bypasses the body is simply a fantasy.

Here are some examples of micro steps that matter deeply in real-life transformation:

- **Emotional Healing:** Taking five minutes daily to notice what you're feeling without judgment. Practicing self-validation. Saying, "It's okay to feel this way."

- **Business Building:** Writing one blog post. Making one offer. Talking about your work to one person.

- **Calling in Love:** Clearing a drawer for your future partner. Practicing receiving with ease from friends. Saying no to people who feel like your past.

- **Creative Projects:** Doodling for fun. Singing aloud in the car. Writing one page of your book, not because it's perfect but because it's yours.

Each of these micro steps is a turn of the wheel in the direction of your future. Each one sends a signal: "I am readying myself. I am preparing the ground."

So, let your life bloom gently. An oak tree doesn't race to grow. The butterfly doesn't rip itself out of the cocoon. The moon doesn't rush to fullness. Nature moves in micro steps, and she always arrives. You are part of that same universal energy.

Let your life unfold in a way that honors your body, your pace, your healing.

Let your revolution be gentle, and your success to be sustainable. Let your next chapter be crafted one micro step at a time.

JOURNAL PROMPT:

List five micro steps that feel like movement toward what you want and comfortable for your nervous system. Revisit this prompt often as your movement toward your goals, and your capacity, expand over time.

At this potent crossroads, the answer is not to sprint toward the next mountain. The most fertile soil for manifestation is not urgent. It's openness, playfulness, and wonder.

joyful becoming: manifestation beyond the wound

There comes a sacred moment in the healing journey when you look around and realize something extraordinary has happened: The trauma no longer holds the reins of your life. The storm has passed. You can still recall it, but you're no longer trapped inside it. Your body breathes easier. Your mind no longer loops in survival. And your heart? It begins to whisper again, not in panic, but in possibility.

When you've reached this place, you've arrived at the edge of something powerful. You're no longer reconstructing your sense of self from the wreckage. Now, you are sculpting from light. You're finally free to build. Not just recover and not just cope—but *create*. And this is the energy of joyful becoming.

But here's the sacred paradox: Even at this potent crossroads, the answer is *not* to sprint toward the next mountain. The most fertile soil for manifestation is not urgency. It's *openness*. It's *playfulness*. It's *wonder*. It's the energy of the child who twirls in a field, making wishes on dandelions without wondering how it will happen, just knowing it *will*.

So, don't rush. Don't force. Just stay open.

Once your subconscious has made its leap out of trauma's grip, and your mind begins defaulting to the possibility rather than constriction, there is a delicious space filled with the buzz of possibility.

From here, many are tempted to rush. To try and "make up for lost time." But manifestation doesn't bloom from pressure. It blooms from presence. It blooms from the breath between the thoughts, the way sunlight invites a bud to open, not by pushing it open but by warming it patiently until it *chooses* to blossom.

In this space, your job is simple: Keep your energy joyful and your desires general. Stay in the field of what feels good. Stay in the energy of wonder and trust, of joy and gratitude as your new *way of being*.

These energies (joy, playfulness, and gratitude) aren't just feel-good buzzwords. They are *amplifiers* in the quantum field. They are what tunes your inner frequency to the vast orchestration of creation itself. Think of them as the breeze that helps the sails of your soul catch the right wind. They are what keep you open to *nudges*, those sacred whispers from the Universe that don't shout but whisper: *this way . . . now turn here . . . wait . . . now go.*

This is what I call "the energy of joyful becoming."

When I was navigating my own darkest valley of my divorce, I felt like I had been stripped bare. I didn't recognize the landscape of my life, and I barely recognized myself. Everything I thought would be permanent was dissolving. I was grieving a dream, and all I could do at times was breathe through the ache.

But somewhere in the depths of that grief, I remembered a truth so quiet, it felt like it had wings:

Joy is not something you earn at the end of your healing. It is part of the healing.

Even in the middle of my sorrow, I began to seek out tiny flickers of joy. And certainly not because I felt ready but because I knew I needed to.

Those moments of joy were very "small" in the beginning. Such as a warm cup of tea. A morning when the sunlight fell *just so* on the kitchen floor. A song that made my cells dance. I collected those tiny joys like treasures. Not as a bypass to pain but as a lifeline back to my true self.

Joy doesn't have to be a big deal. Sometimes it's a shimmer. A moment in time.

And those small moments? They stack. Like tiny bricks, they build a whole new foundation. And one day, you realize you're not just feeling better, you're becoming someone new. Someone lighter. Someone freer. Someone open to more.

As you are in this new phase of manifestation, one cautionary heads-up is necessary: One of the most common mistakes in manifestation is becoming so fixated on a specific outcome that you block the blessings trying to reach you in a different form.

Let me explain.

You may have your heart set on something very particular. For example's sake, let's say a relationship with a specific person. Let's call him Bob. You've imagined it, written about it, maybe even manifested parts of it. But here's the truth: You can't manifest *Bob*, because Bob has free will. You can't manifest *that exact job title*, *that exact apartment*, or *that exact scenario* down to the last detail.

But what you *can* manifest is the *feeling* you wanted in that relationship, job, or apartment. You can manifest integrity, connection, safety, joy, love, support, freedom.

And so maybe, after all your inner work, after aligning with joy and gratitude, Bob doesn't show up. But John does. And with John, you feel seen. You feel cherished. You feel safe to be exactly who you are.

Does it matter if it's John instead of Bob? Not if the essence of what you desired is there.

This is why specificity in *emotion* matters far more than specificity in *form*. The more general your manifestation focus is, and the more it is rooted in feeling rather than form, the more room the Universe has to conspire with you to make it happen.

Think of it like telling the GPS you want to go somewhere warm, relaxing, and by the water. If you input *exactly* "this beach house, on this street, with this furniture," you might miss the lakeside cabin that was even more aligned for you. You narrow the road so much, you choke out the detours that would've led you *home*.

So, stay curious, not controlling. Stay wonder-filled, not rigid. The path of joyful becoming is marked by your willingness to both dream and surrender at the same time. This is how you stay in the manifestation mind: by defaulting to openness, not attachment.

When you release the grip on exactly how something must look, you invite in the truth of what you really want: the experience of being fully alive, fully supported, and headed for fulfillment from the inside out.

This process is not just about getting what you want, it's about becoming who you are without the trauma. It's about returning to your wholeness before you had to shrink or mold or survive.

Joyful becoming is a way you move. A way you relate to yourself. A way you cocreate with the infinite. This is the version of you that no longer waits for permission to shine. This is you who laughs more easily, loves more freely, and believes in what's possible. This is you who lets the wind of joy carry you toward the life you deserve.

So please, joyfully dance with the process. Let the days be light. Let your gratitude sing even before the answer arrives.

And a final word from me to you:

Writing this for you, walking this road beside you, even if only through these pages, has been one of the great honors of my life. Thank you for allowing me into your heart, your healing, and your becoming.

May your path be luminous. May your joy be contagious. And may you manifest more than you dared to dream. Not because you forced it but because you remembered that you were always worthy of it.

acknowledgments

Thank you to my clients for partnering with me and trusting me to enter the most vulnerable places in their hearts and minds. You inspired me then, you inspire me today, and I'll continue to be inspired by you for years to come.

Thank you to Andy for being so supportive of this work and coparenting with me so wonderfully that it created space and support to write this book. Your belief in me and my work made a tremendous impact on me. Thank you for your kindness, your friendship, and your encouragement.

Special thanks to the incredible team at fEMPOWER Publications for believing in my message and supporting me as I birthed this book from thoughts to physical reality. I am blessed to have this team and grateful for all of you.

I wouldn't be the person I am without the love and support I'm fortunate to have in my life. I have the best family and support team in the world: my mother, my amazing husband, and my sister-friend Nicole. Thank you for your devotion, support, and guidance when I bring projects to life.

Love, Diane

At fEMPOWER Publications,
we don't just publish books—we amplify movements.

We support thought leaders, visionary storytellers, and creative entrepreneurs
in transforming their ideas into powerful nonfiction books, journals, workbooks,
affirmation decks, and personal growth tools that leave lasting impact.

Our mission is to help our authors protect their soul's work, expand HER
platform beyond the page, and turn HER message into a timeless legacy.

www.fempower.pub | @fempower.pub ⊚

www.ingramcontent.com/pod-product-compliance
Lightning Source LLC
Chambersburg PA
CBHW051307120626
46547CB00015B/2127

* 9 7 8 1 9 9 8 7 2 1 2 4 5 *